101 Inspirational Coloring Patterns
COLORING BOOK
Currated by Todd Cotton

---

*"No matter how much we grow taller, grow older,
we are still forever stumbling...forever wondering, forever young.*

This publication is part of a series of products and publications.
For more information, please visit: **http://www.101bookclub.com.**

"101 Book Club" is a subsidiary of
Top of the Nation Enterprises, Inc.

REMEMBER NO ONE CAN MAKE YOU FEEL INFERIOR WITHOUT YOUR CONSENT.

Eleanor Roosevelt

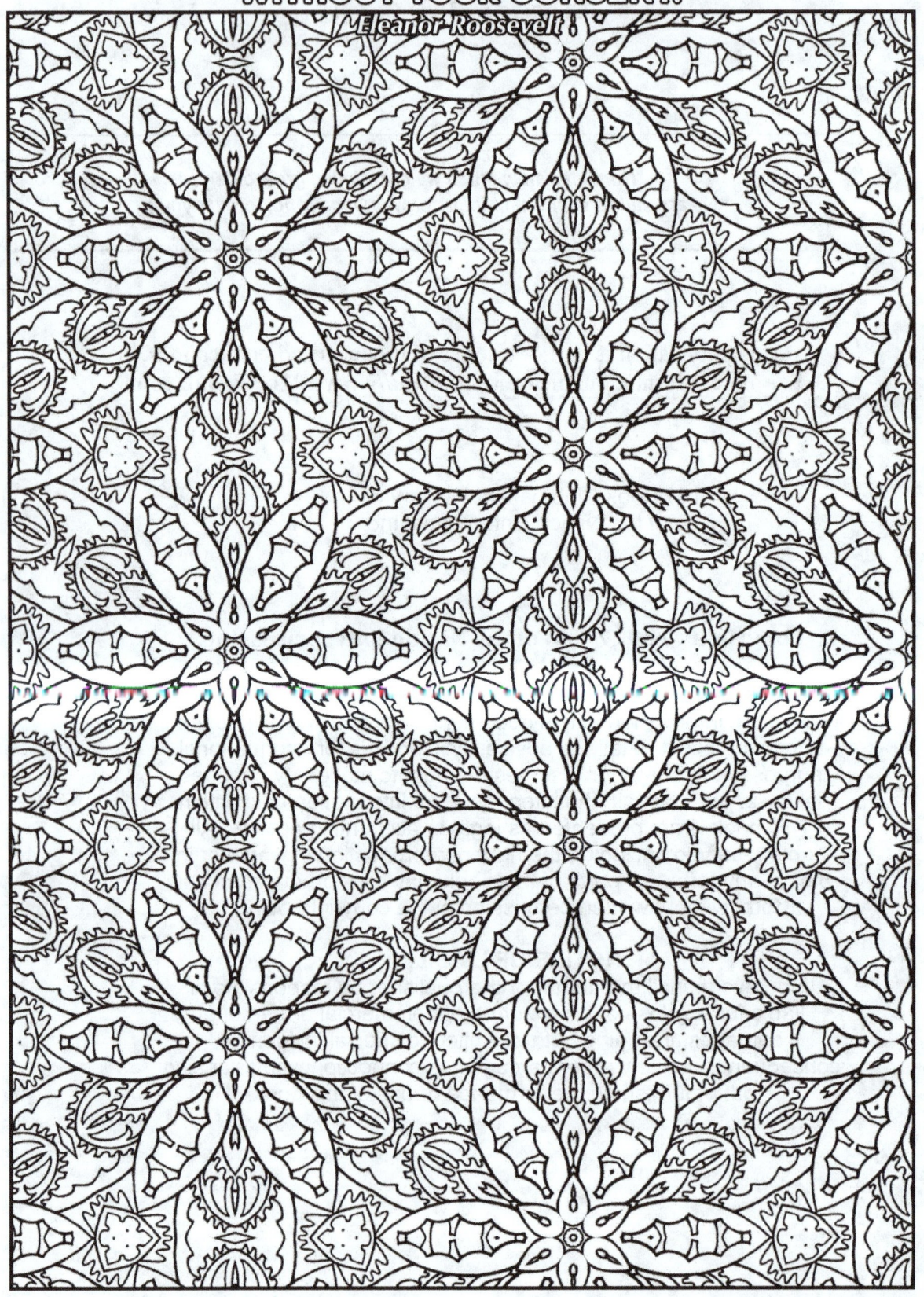

EDUCATION COSTS MONEY.
BUT THEN SO DOES IGNORANCE . . .
Sir Claus Moser

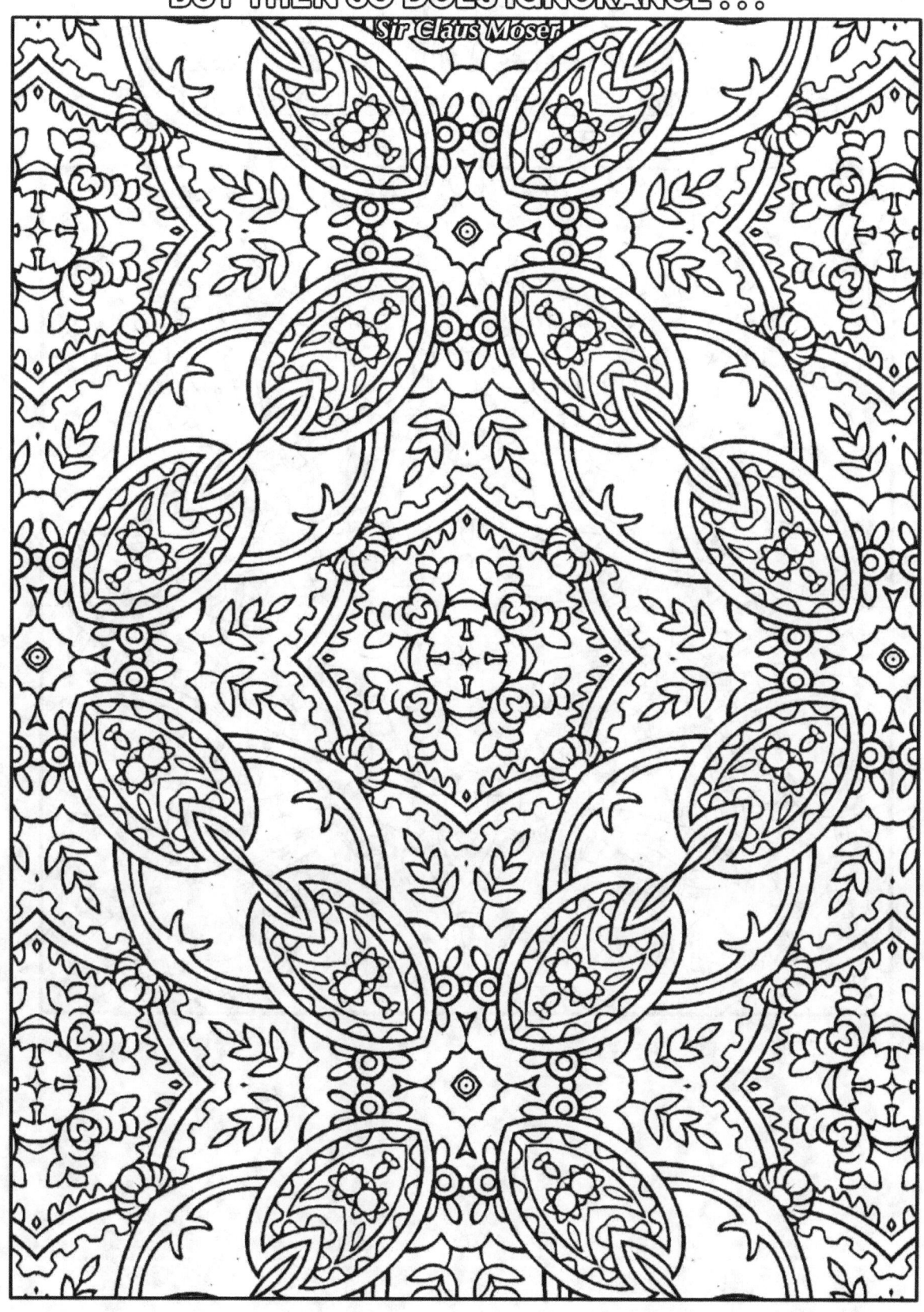

THE BATTLES THAT COUNT
AREN'T THE ONES FOR GOLD MEDALS.
THE STRUGGLES WITHIN YOURSELF
THE INVISIBLE BATTLES INSIDE ALL OF US
THAT'S WHERE IT'S AT.

Jesse Owens

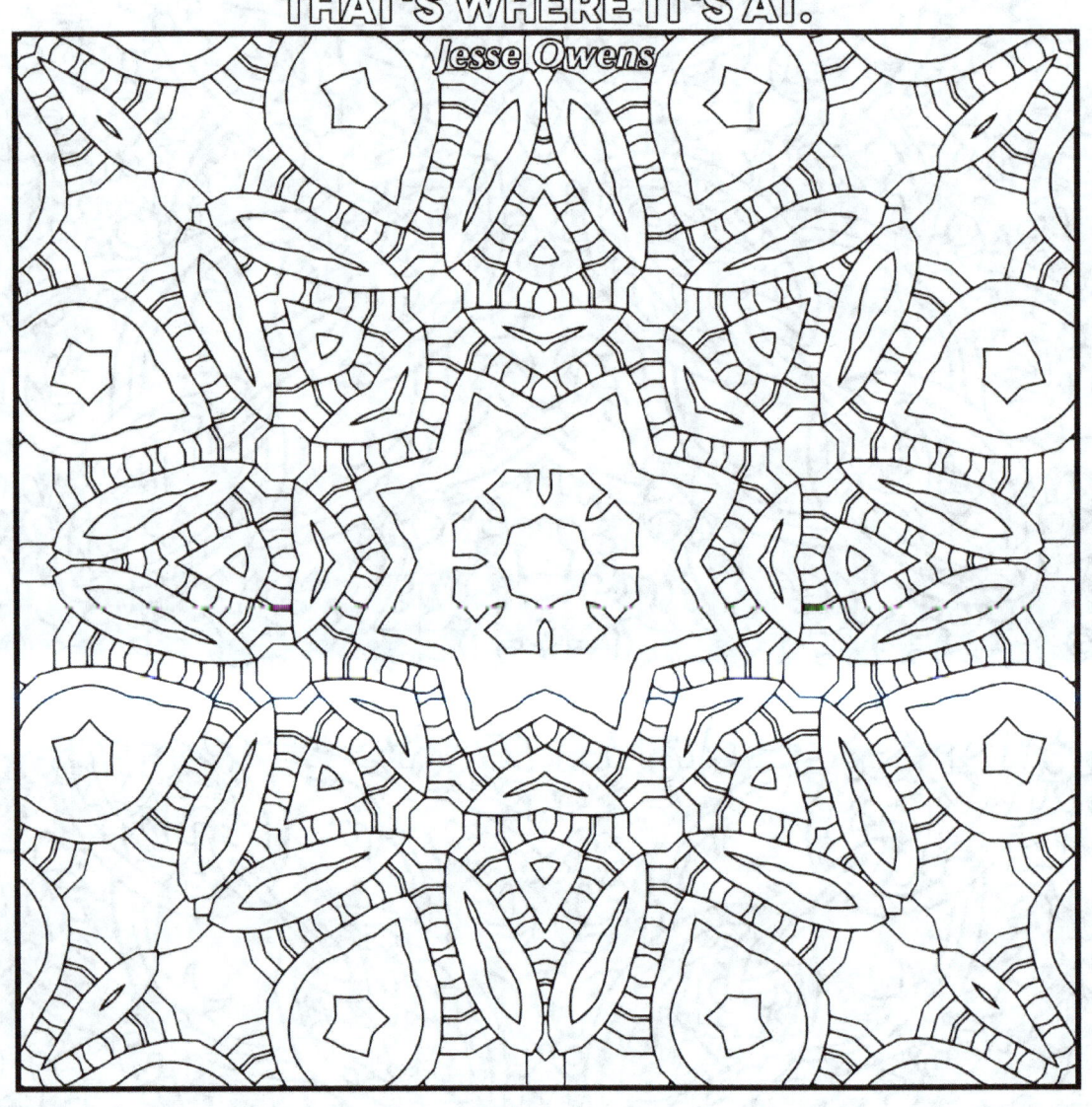

MY MOTHER TOLD ME HAPPINESS WAS THE KEY TO LIFE.
WHEN I WENT TO SCHOOL, THEY ASKED ME
WHAT I WANTED TO BE WHEN I GREW UP.
I WROTE DOWN 'HAPPY'.
THEY TOLD ME I DIDN'T UNDERSTAND THE ASSIGNMENT,
AND I TOLD THEM THEY DIDN'T UNDERSTAND LIFE.
John Lennon

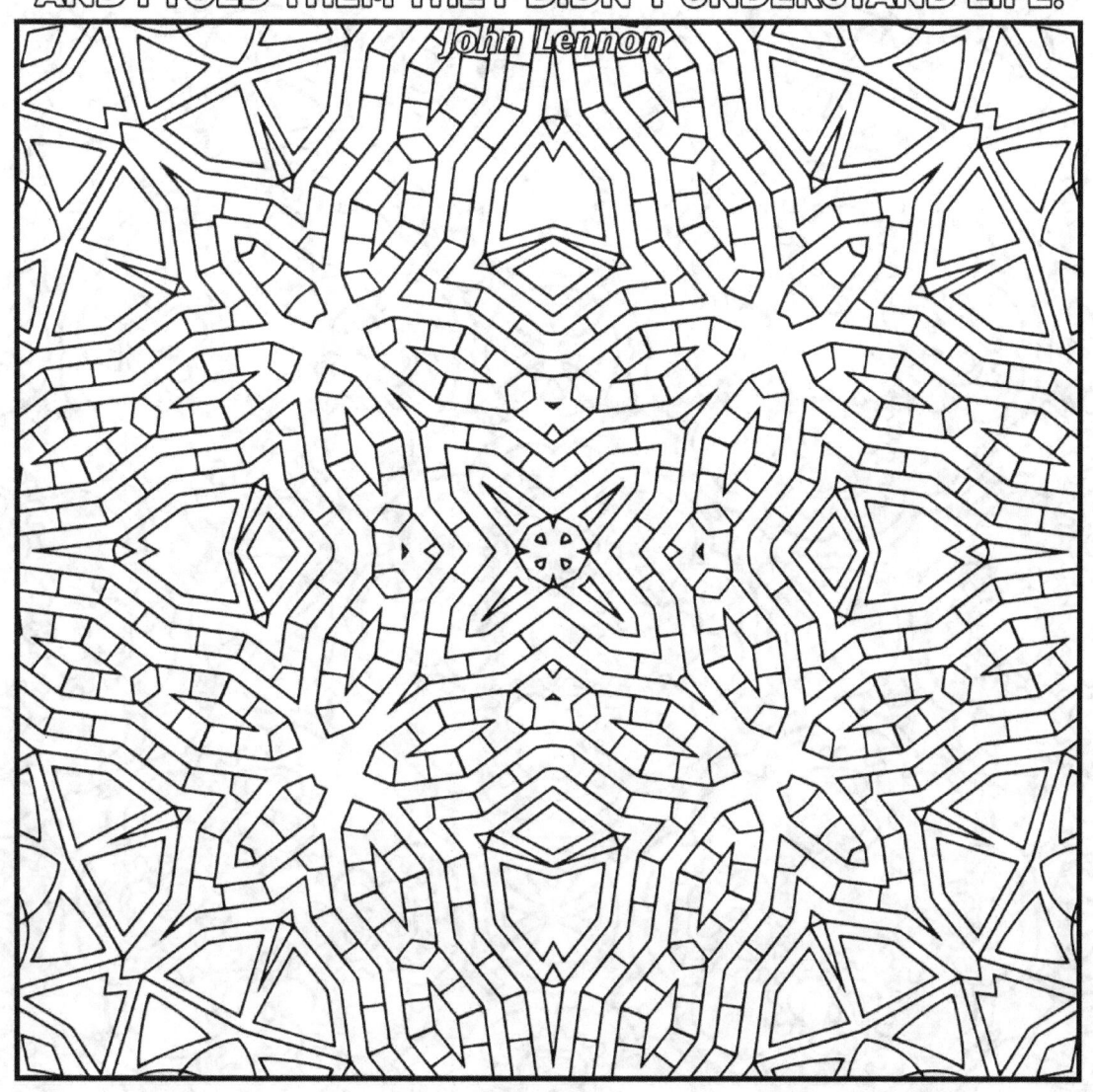

EVERYTHING YOU'VE EVER WANTED
IS ON THE OTHER SIDE OF FEAR.
George Addair

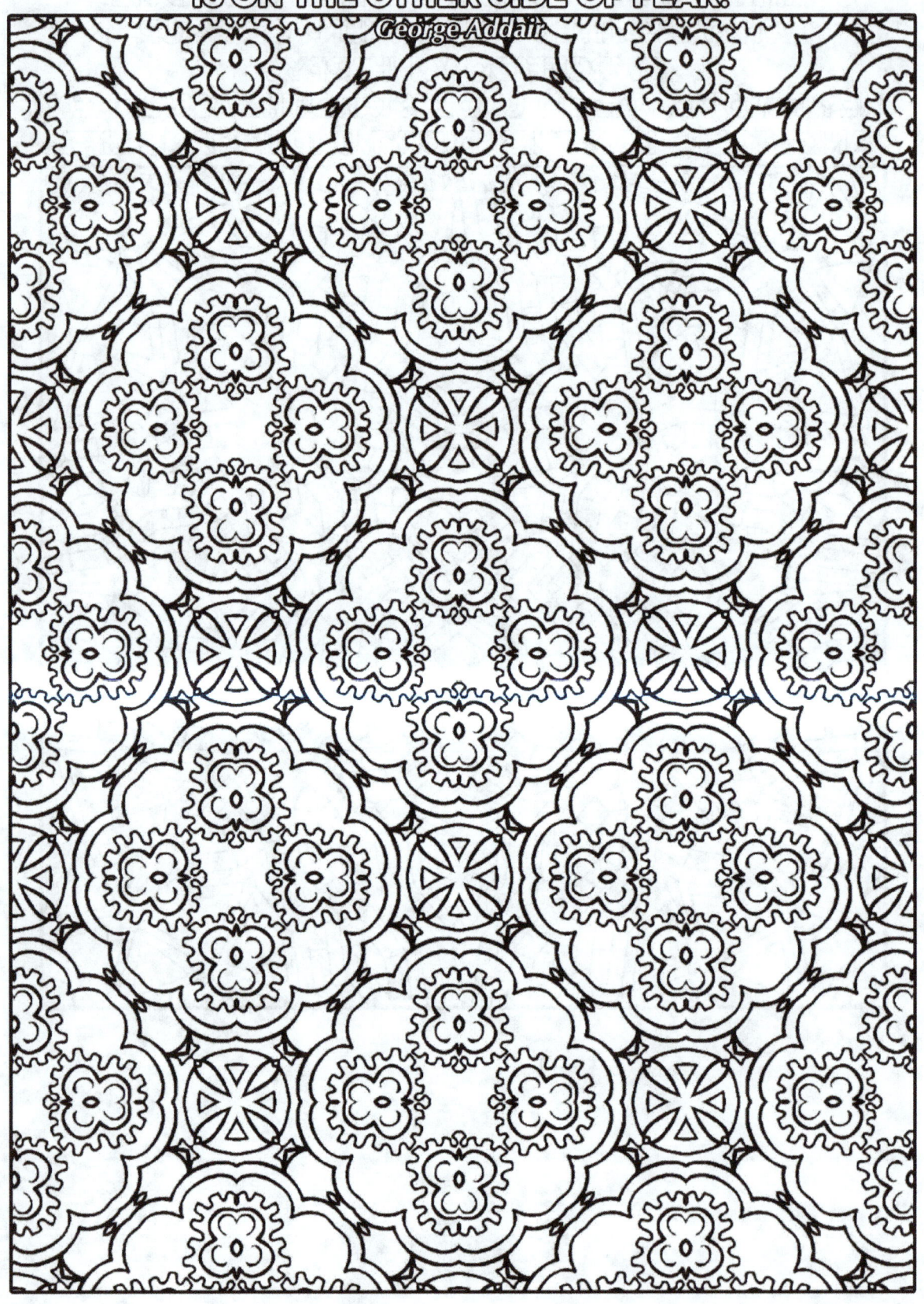

LIFE IS ABOUT MAKING AN IMPACT,
NOT MAKING AN INCOME.

Kevin Kruse

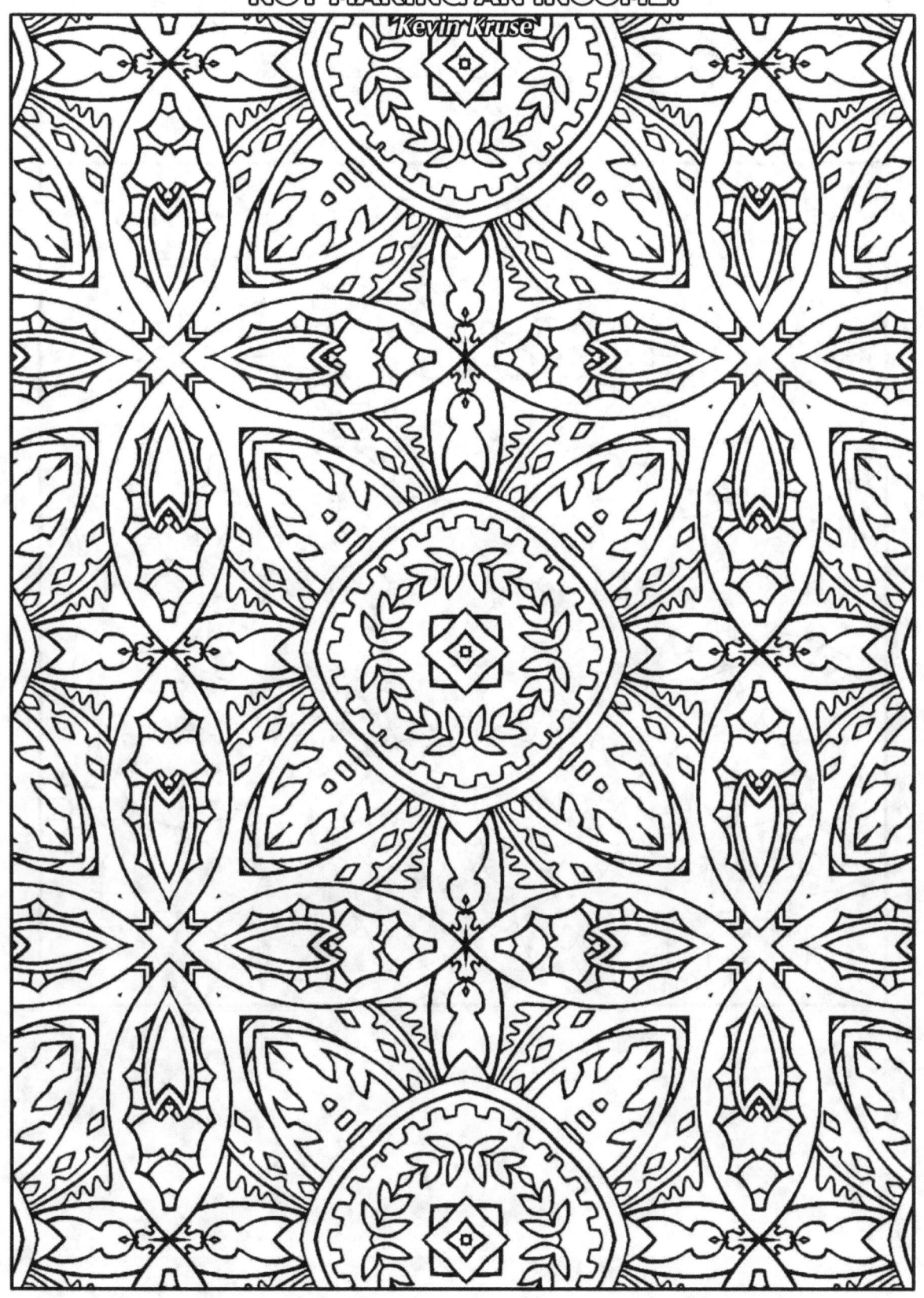

I'VE LEARNED THAT
PEOPLE WILL FORGET, WHAT YOU SAID,
PEOPLE WILL FORGET WHAT YOU DID,
BUT PEOPLE WILL NEVER FORGET
HOW YOU MADE THEM FEEL.
Maya Angelou

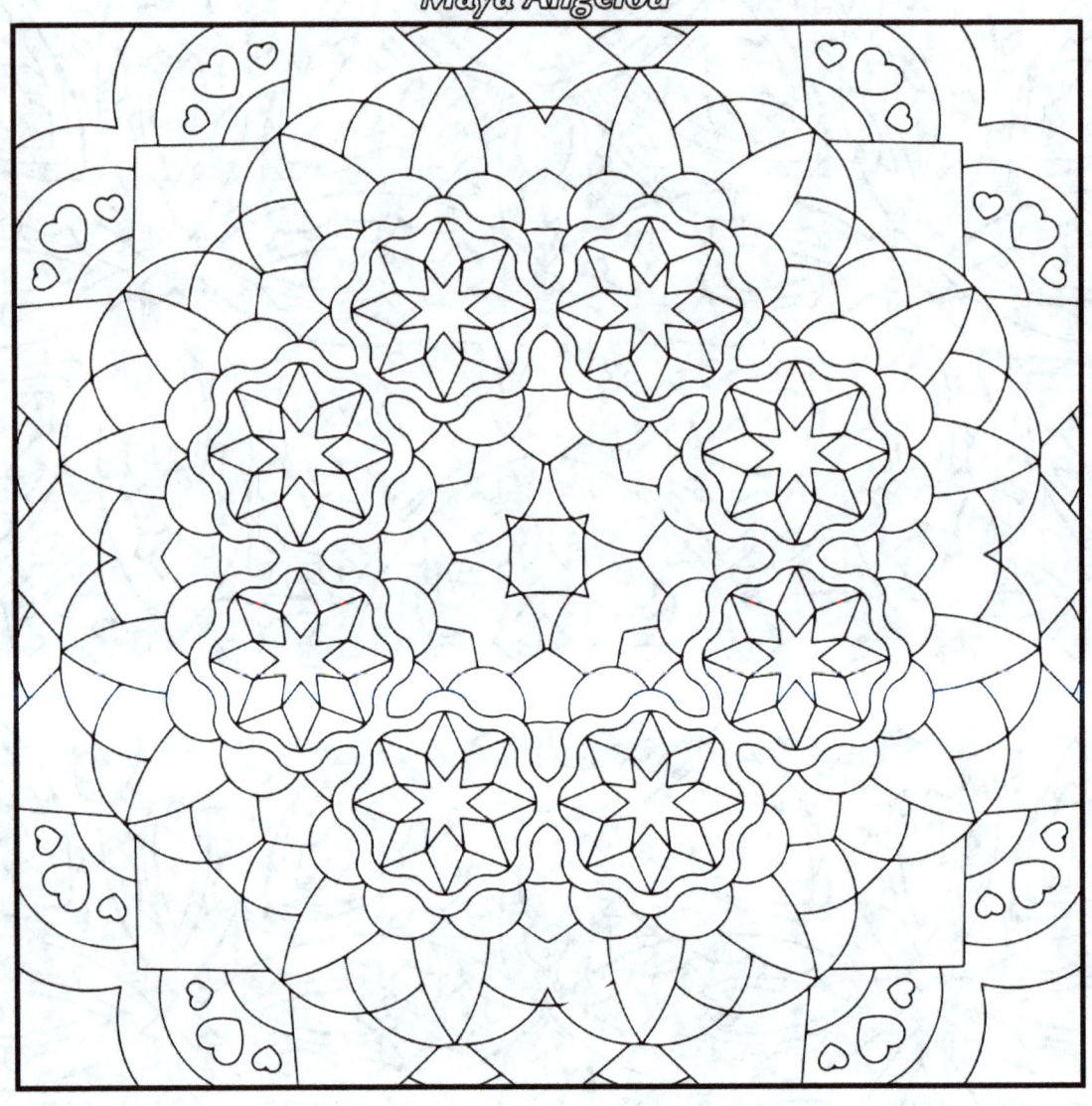

TWENTY YEARS FROM NOW
YOU WILL BE MORE DISAPPOINTED BY THE THINGS
THAT YOU DIDN'T DO THAN BY THE ONES YOU DID DO,
SO THROW OFF THE BOWLINES,
SAIL AWAY FROM SAFE HARBOR,
CATCH THE TRADE WINDS IN YOUR SAILS.
EXPLORE, DREAM, DISCOVER.
Mark Twain

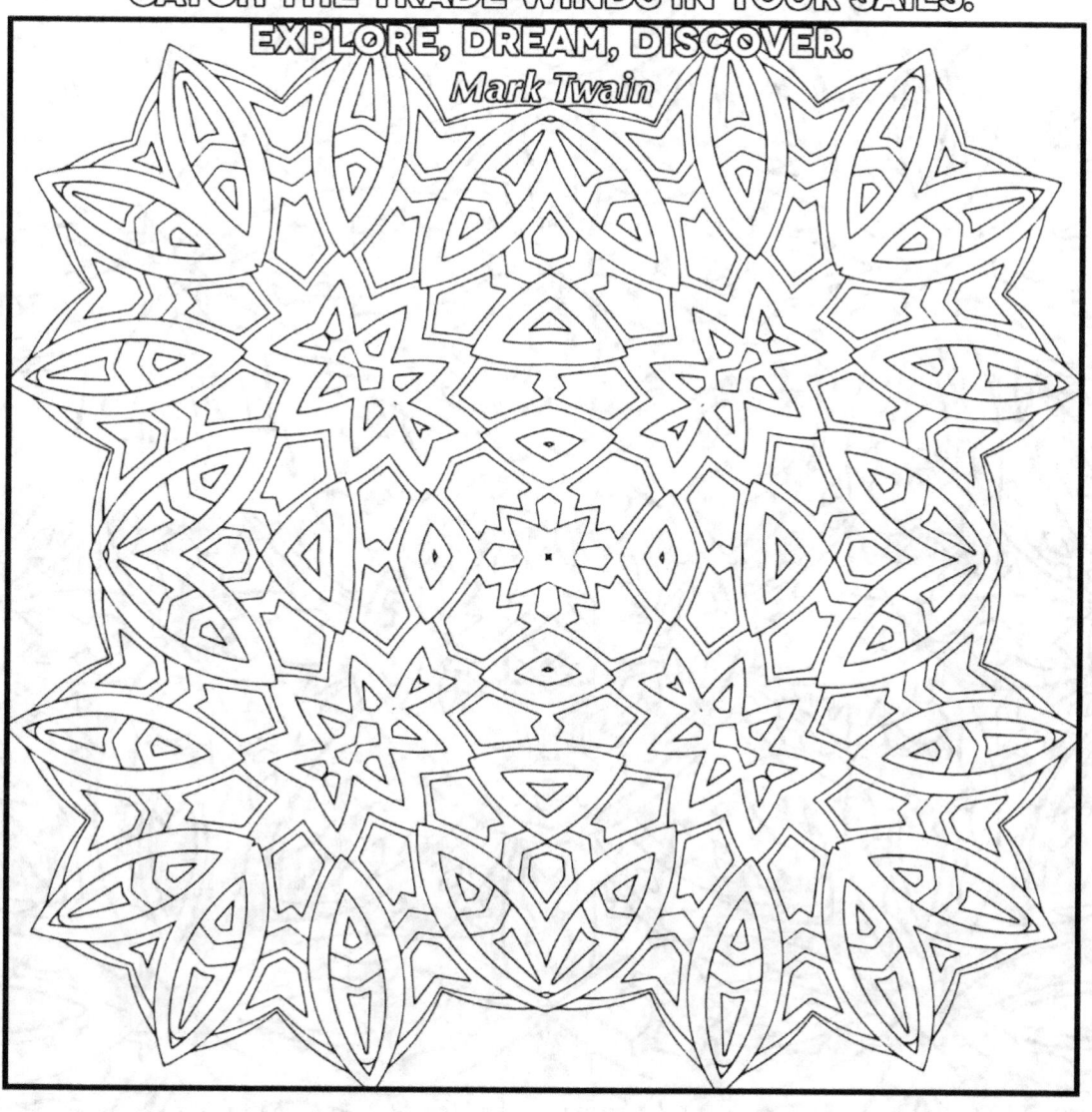

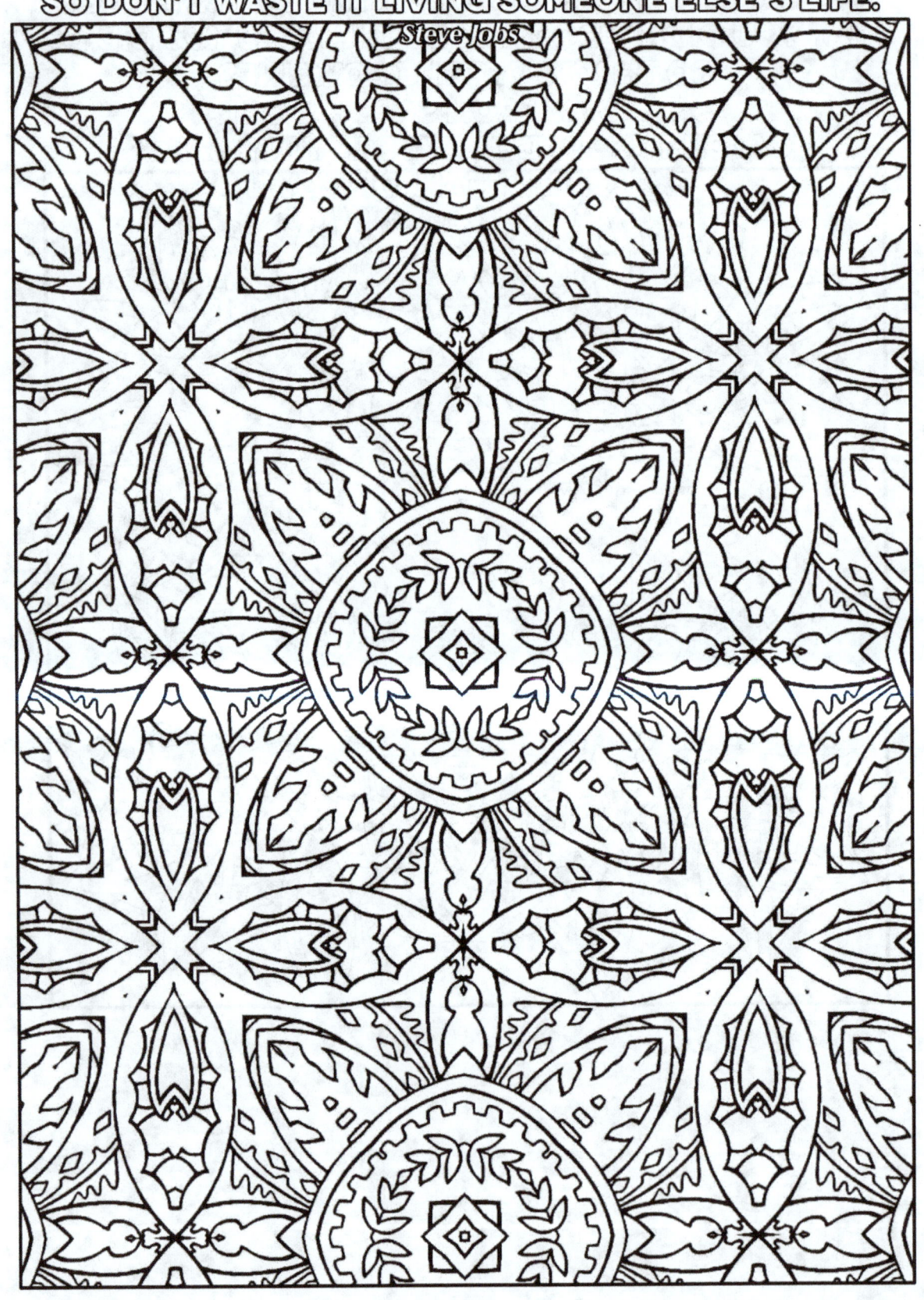

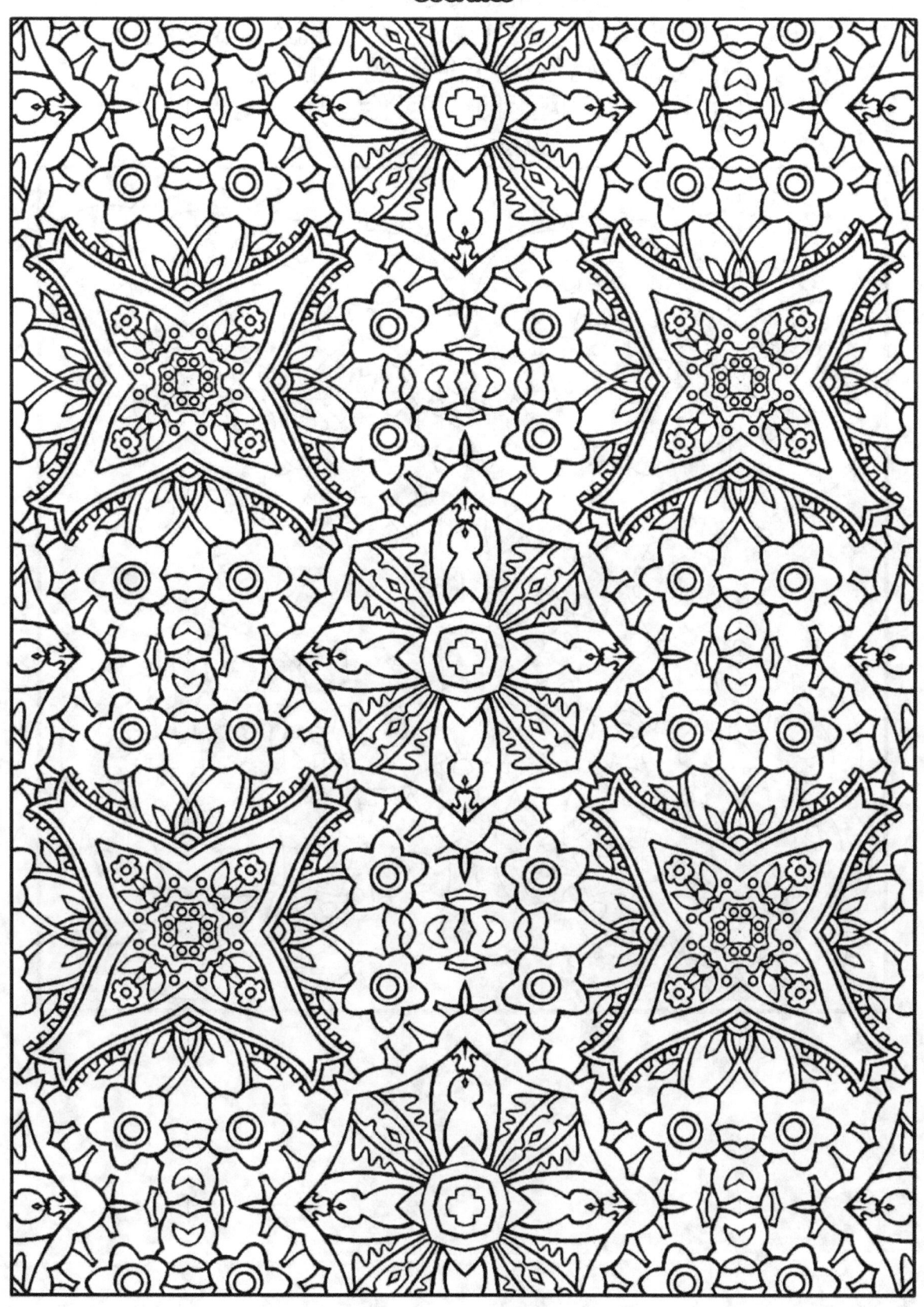

WHEN ONE DOOR OF HAPPINESS CLOSES,
ANOTHER OPENS,
BUT OFTEN WE LOOK SO LONG AT THE CLOSED DOOR
THAT WE DO NOT SEE THE ONE
THAT HAS BEEN OPENED FOR US.
Helen Keller

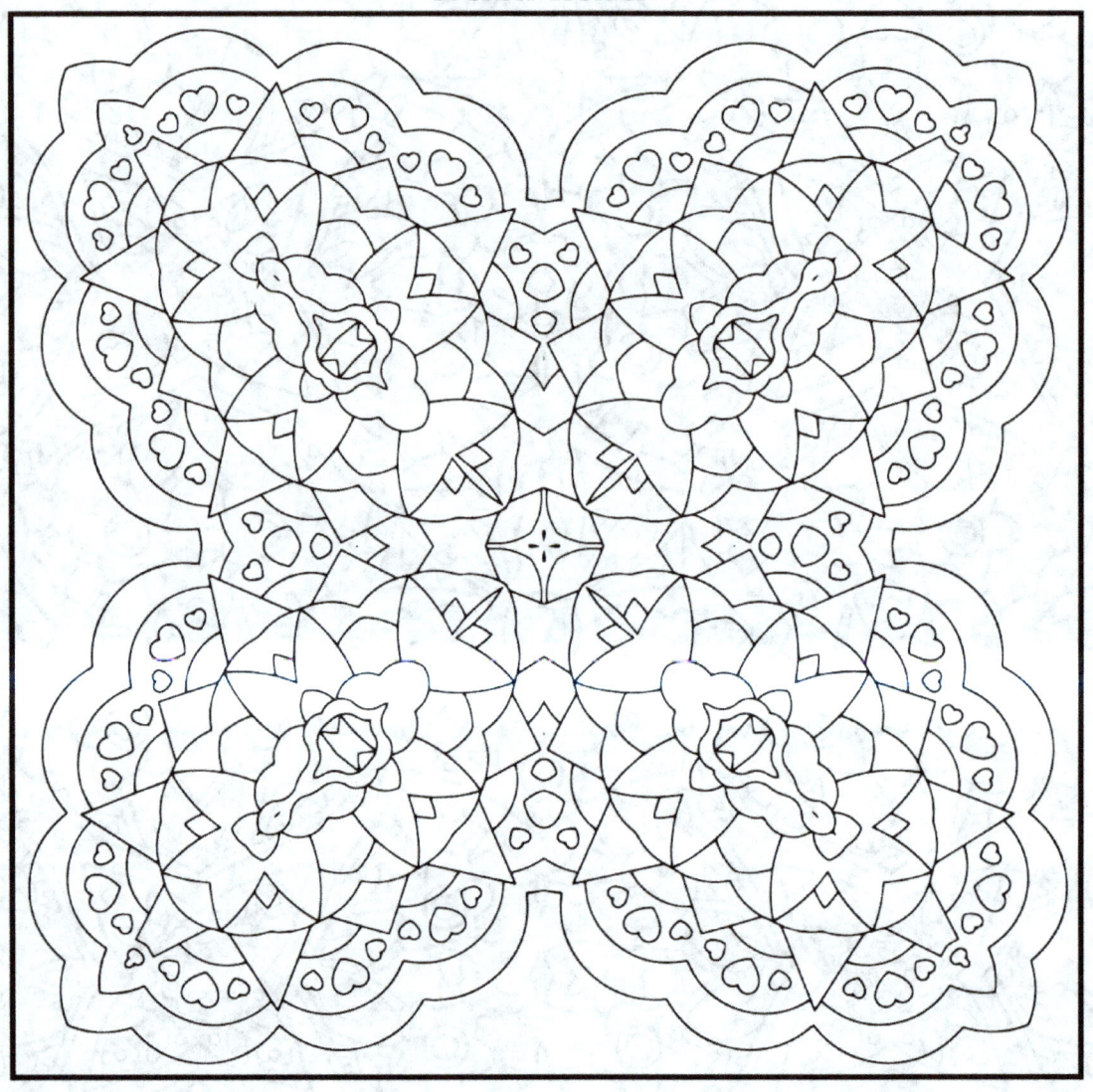

IT IS NOT WHAT YOU DO FOR YOUR CHILDREN,
BUT WHAT YOU HAVE TAUGHT THEM
TO DO FOR THEMSELVES,
THAT WILL MAKE THEM
SUCCESSFUL HUMAN BEINGS.
Ann Landers

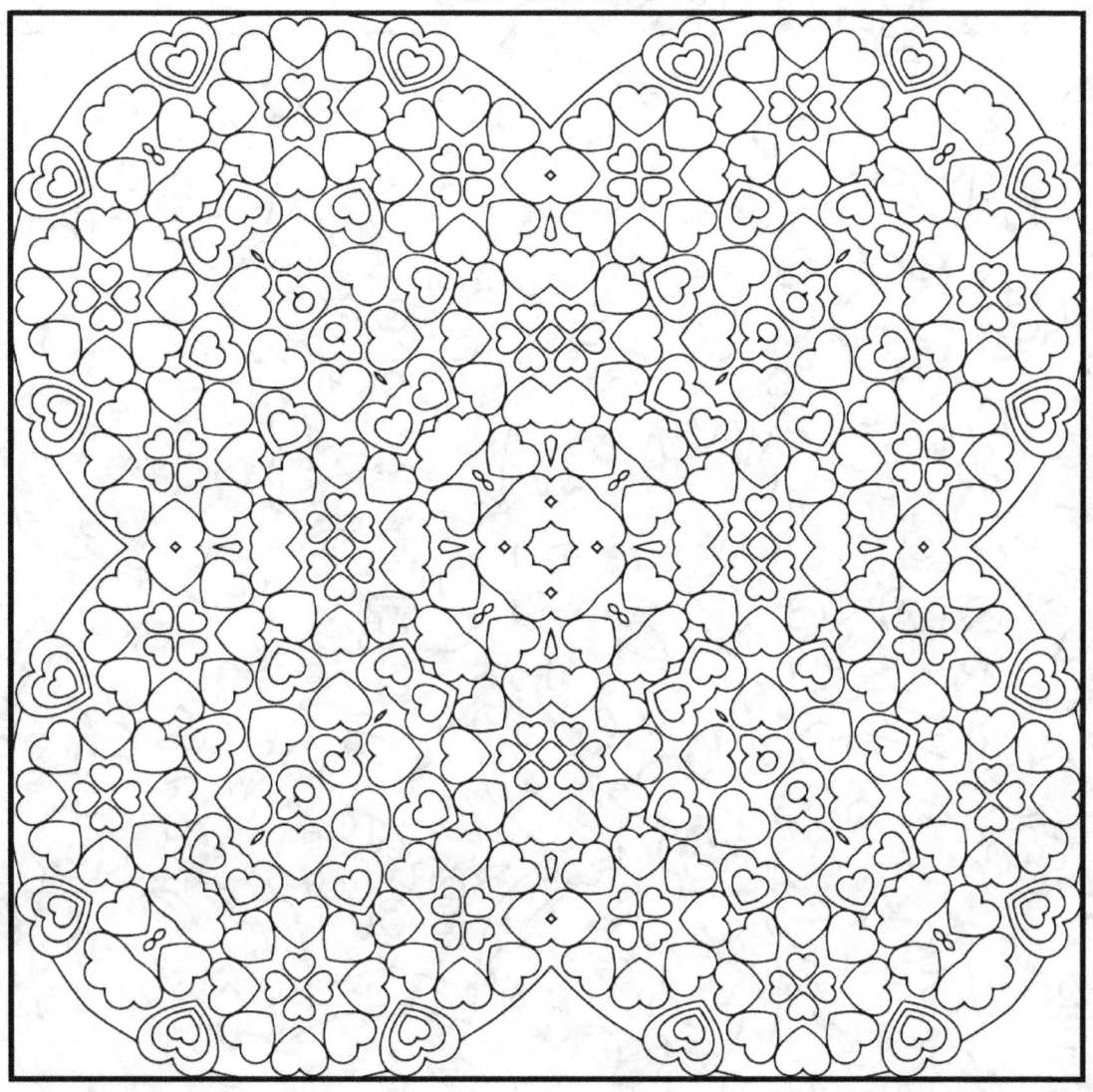

I WOULD RATHER DIE OF PASSION THAN OF BOREDOM
Vincent van Gogh

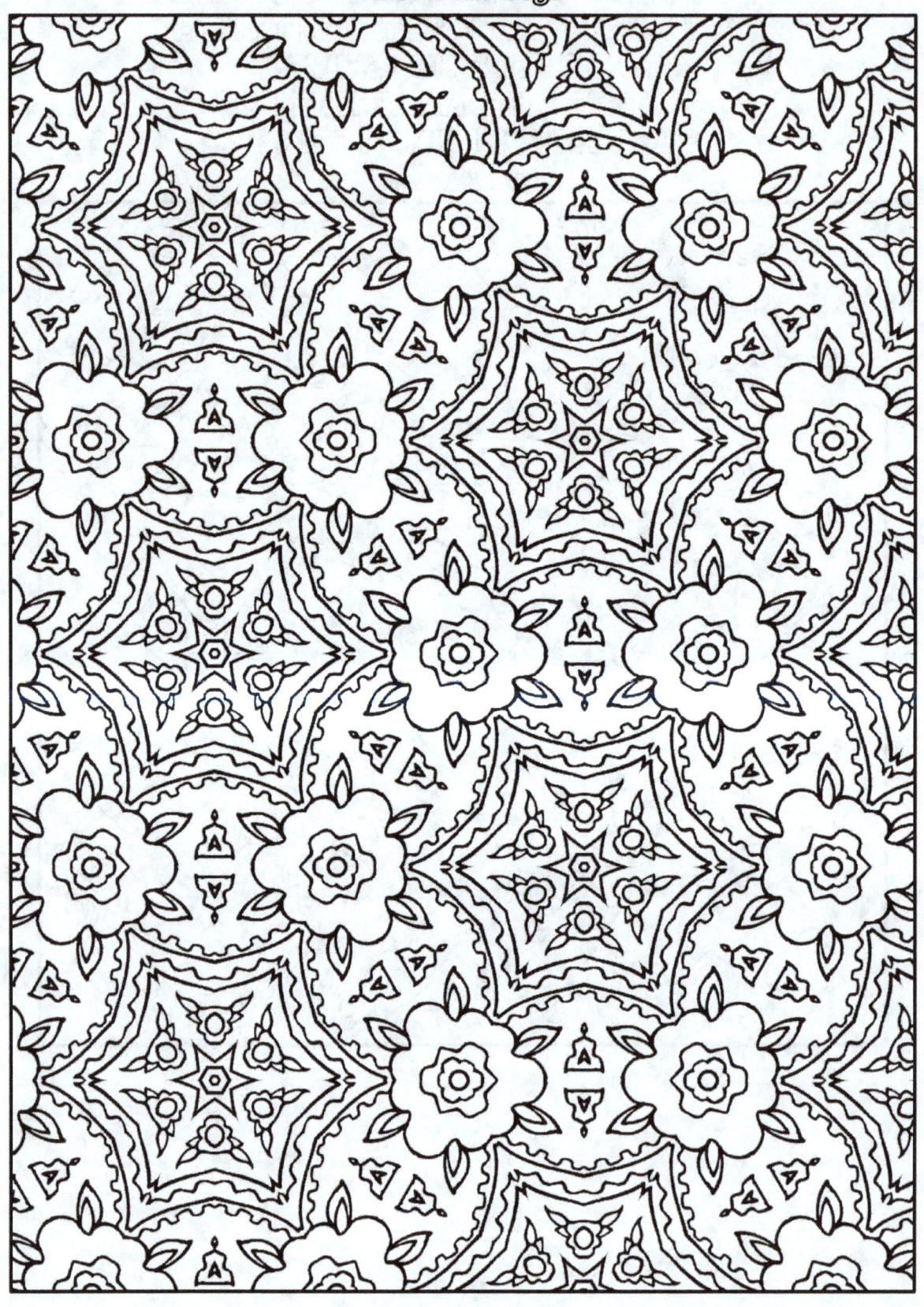

A PERSON WHO NEVER MADE A MISTAKE
NEVER TRIED ANYTHING NEW.
Albert Einstein

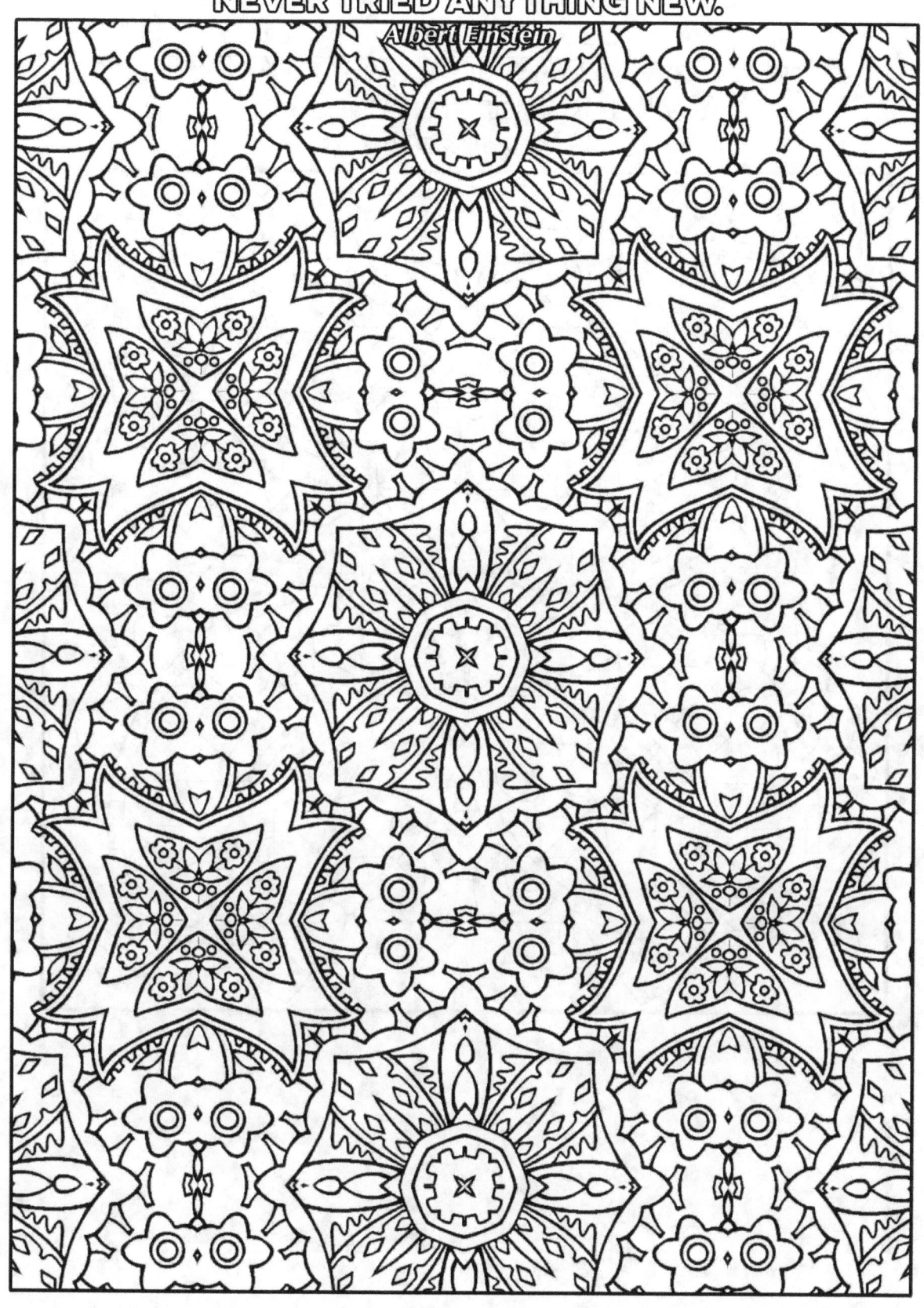

**IF YOU LOOK AT WHAT YOU HAVE IN LIFE,
YOU'LL ALWAYS HAVE MORE.
IF YOU LOOK AT WHAT YOU DON'T HAVE IN LIFE,
YOU'LL NEVER HAVE ENOUGH.**
Oprah Winfrey

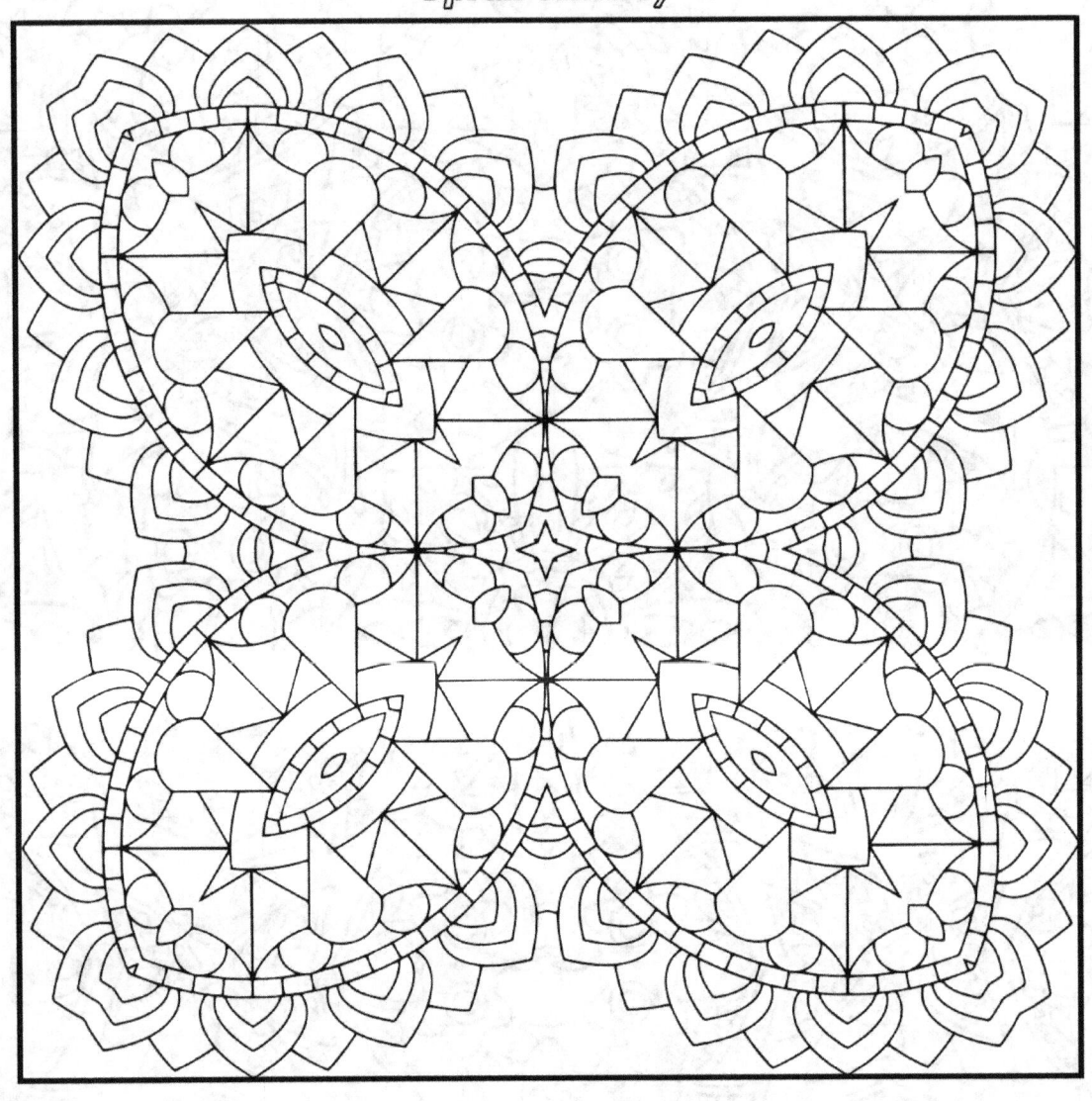

WHEN EVERYTHING SEEMS TO BE GOING AGAINST YOU,
REMEMBER THAT THE AIRPLANE TAKES OFF
AGAINST THE WIND,
NOT WITH IT.
Henry Ford

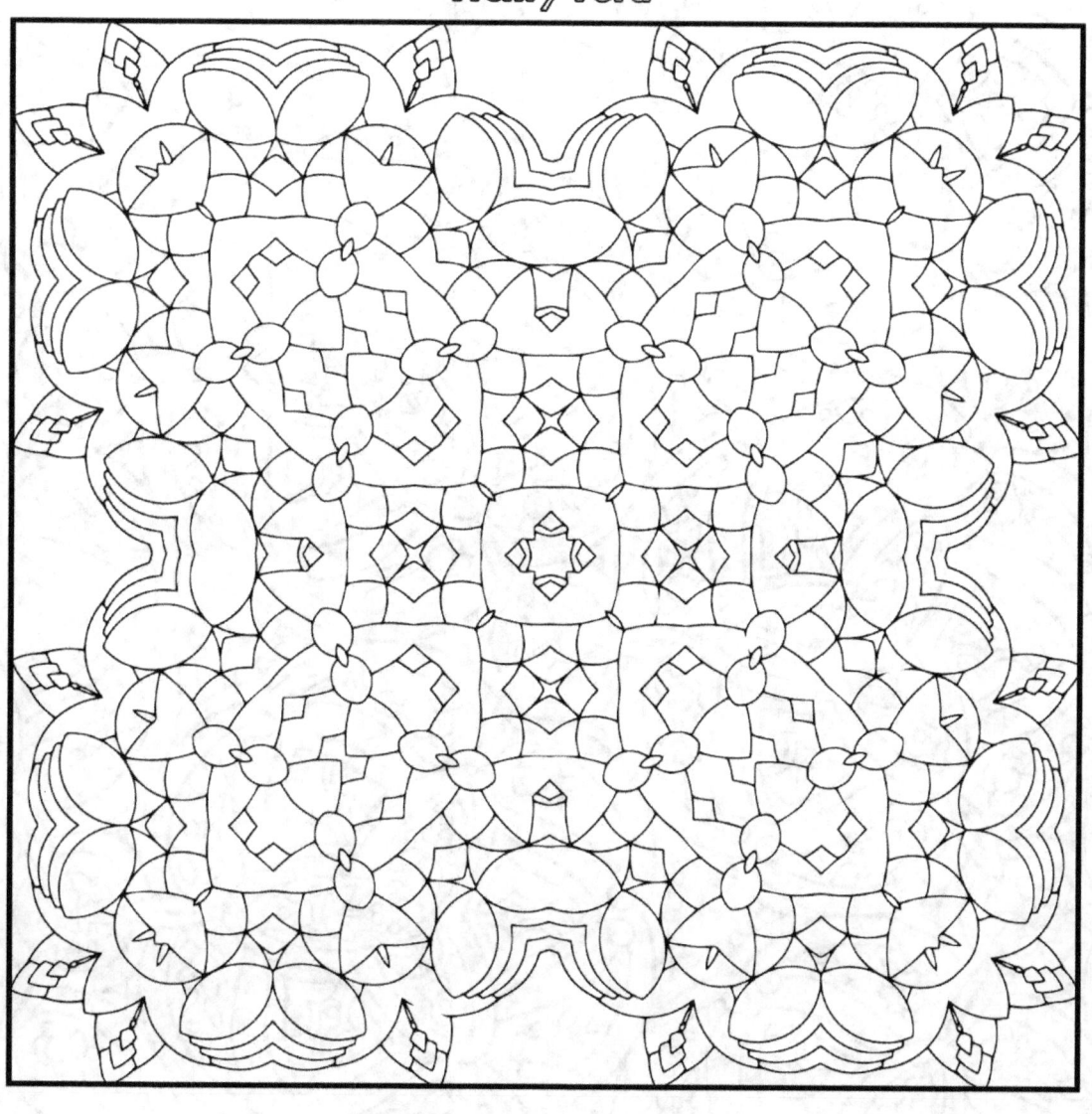

IF YOU CAN DREAM IT, YOU CAN ACHIEVE IT.
Zig Ziglar

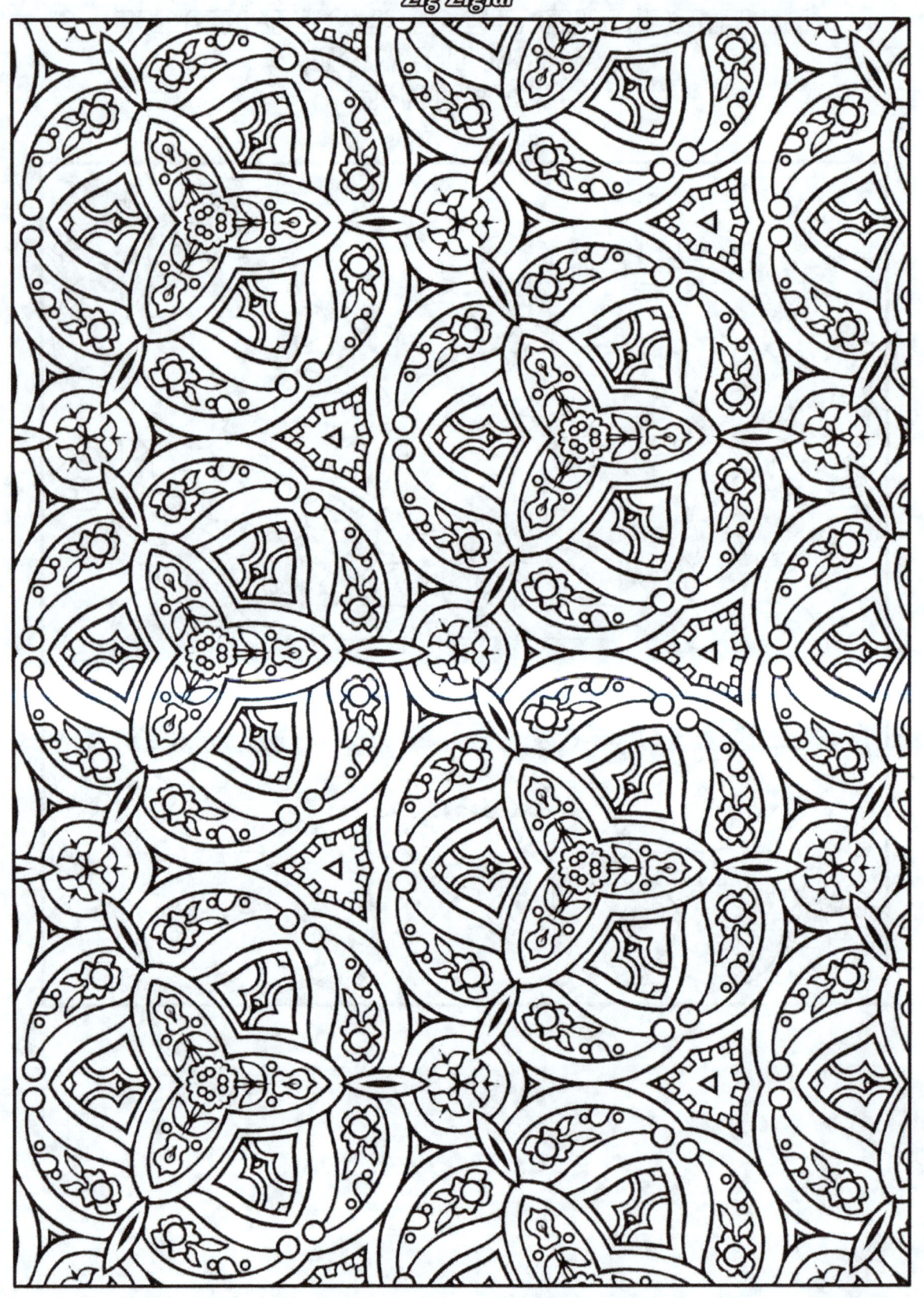

THERE ARE NO TRAFFIC JAMS ALONG THE EXTRA MILE
Roger Staubach

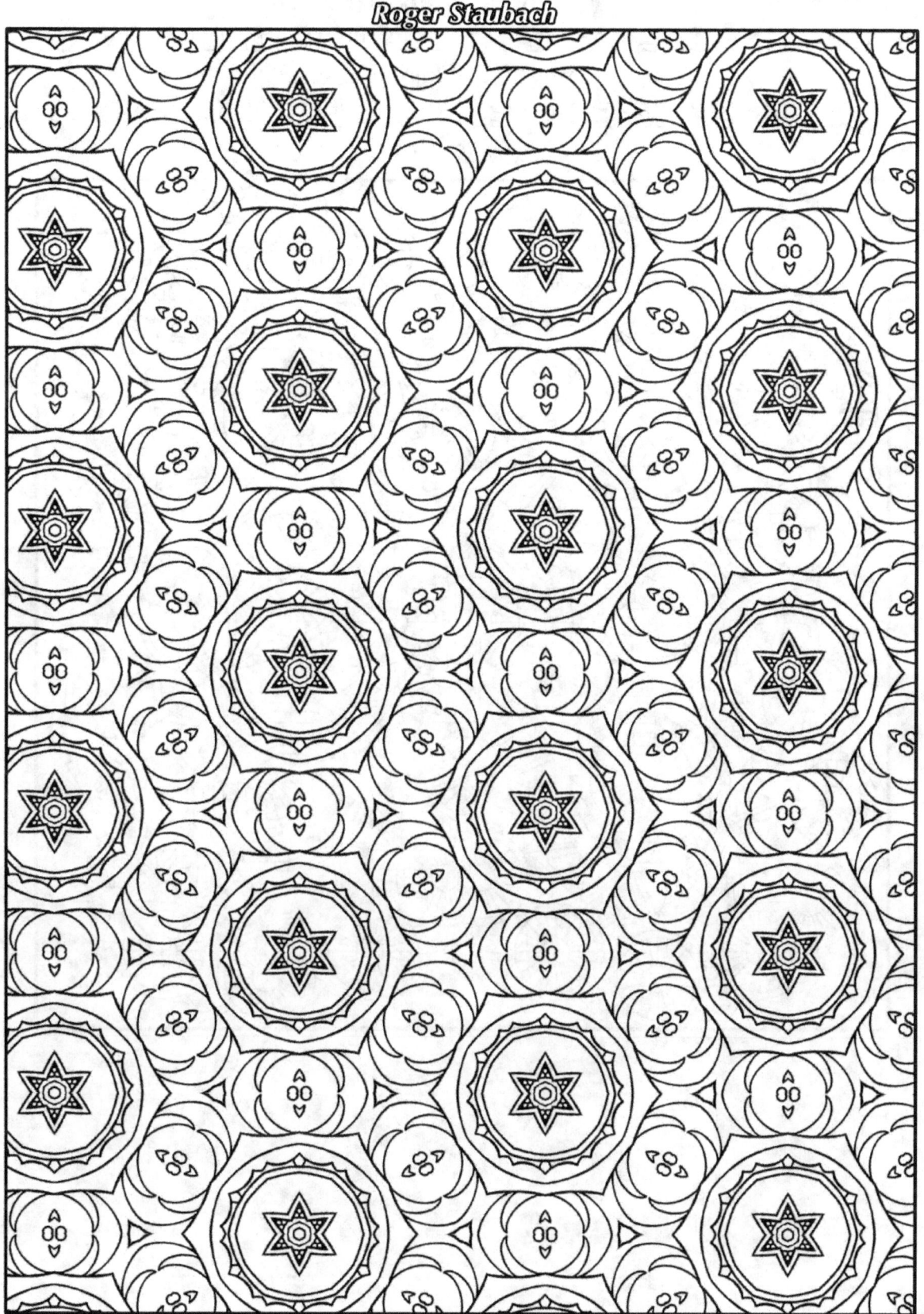

WHAT'S MONEY?
A MAN IS A SUCCESS IF HE GETS UP IN THE MORNING
AND GOES TO BED AT NIGHT
AND IN BETWEEN DOES WHAT HE WANTS TO DO.
Bob Dylan

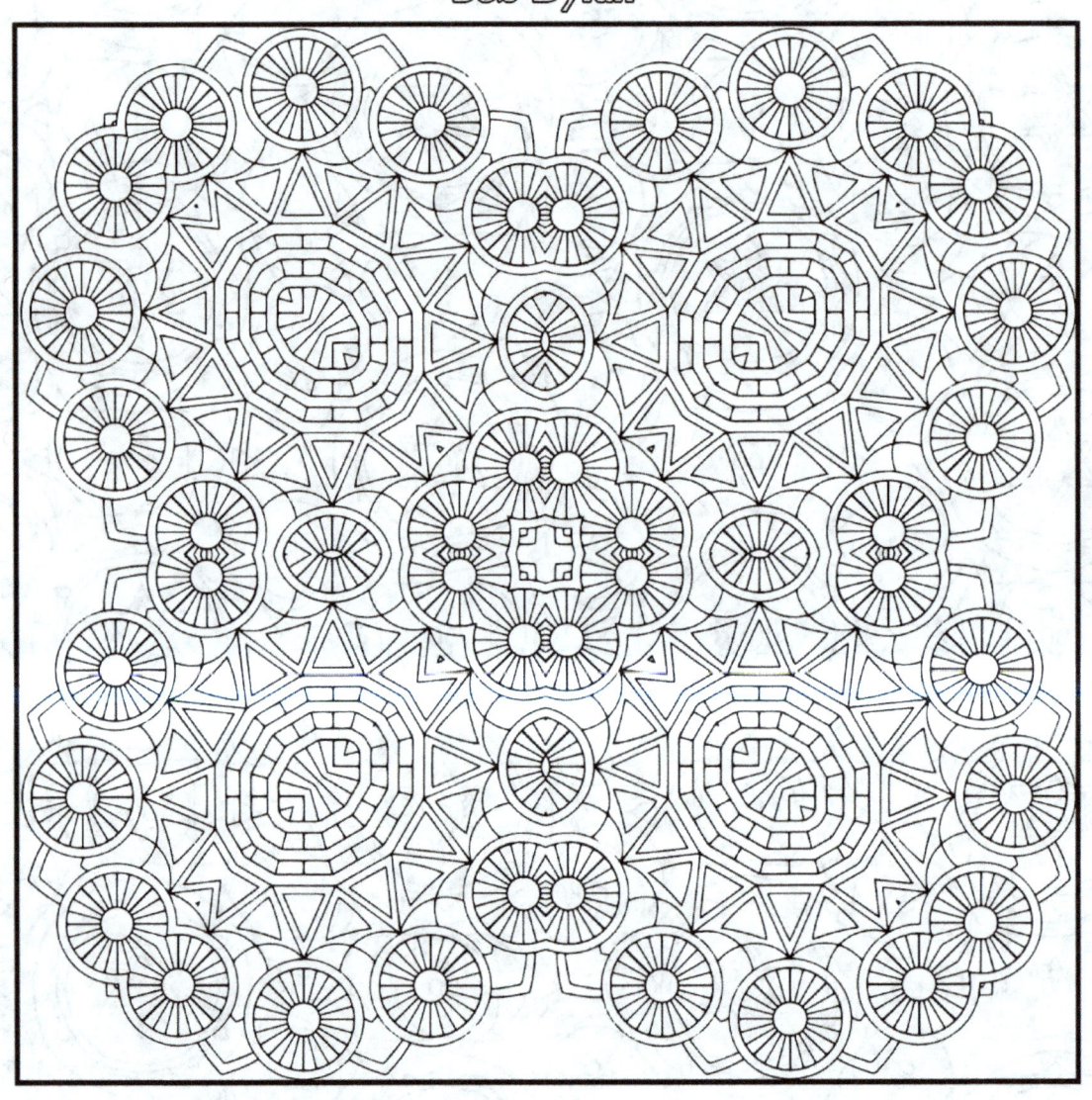

I HAVE BEEN IMPRESSED WITH THE URGENCY OF DOING.
KNOWING IS NOT ENOUGH;
WE MUST APPLY.
BEING WILLING IS NOT ENOUGH;
WE MUST DO.
Leonardo da Vinci

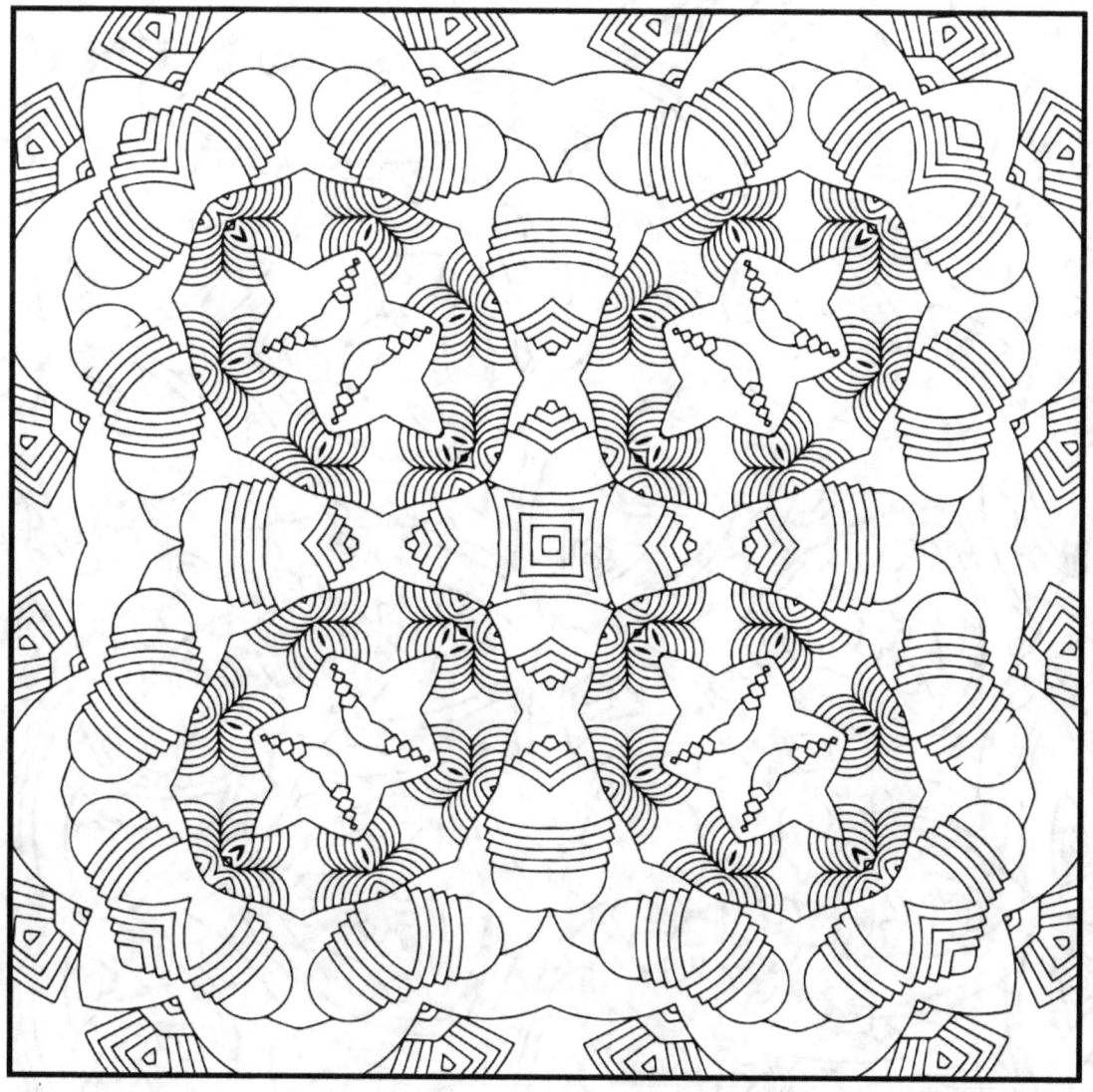

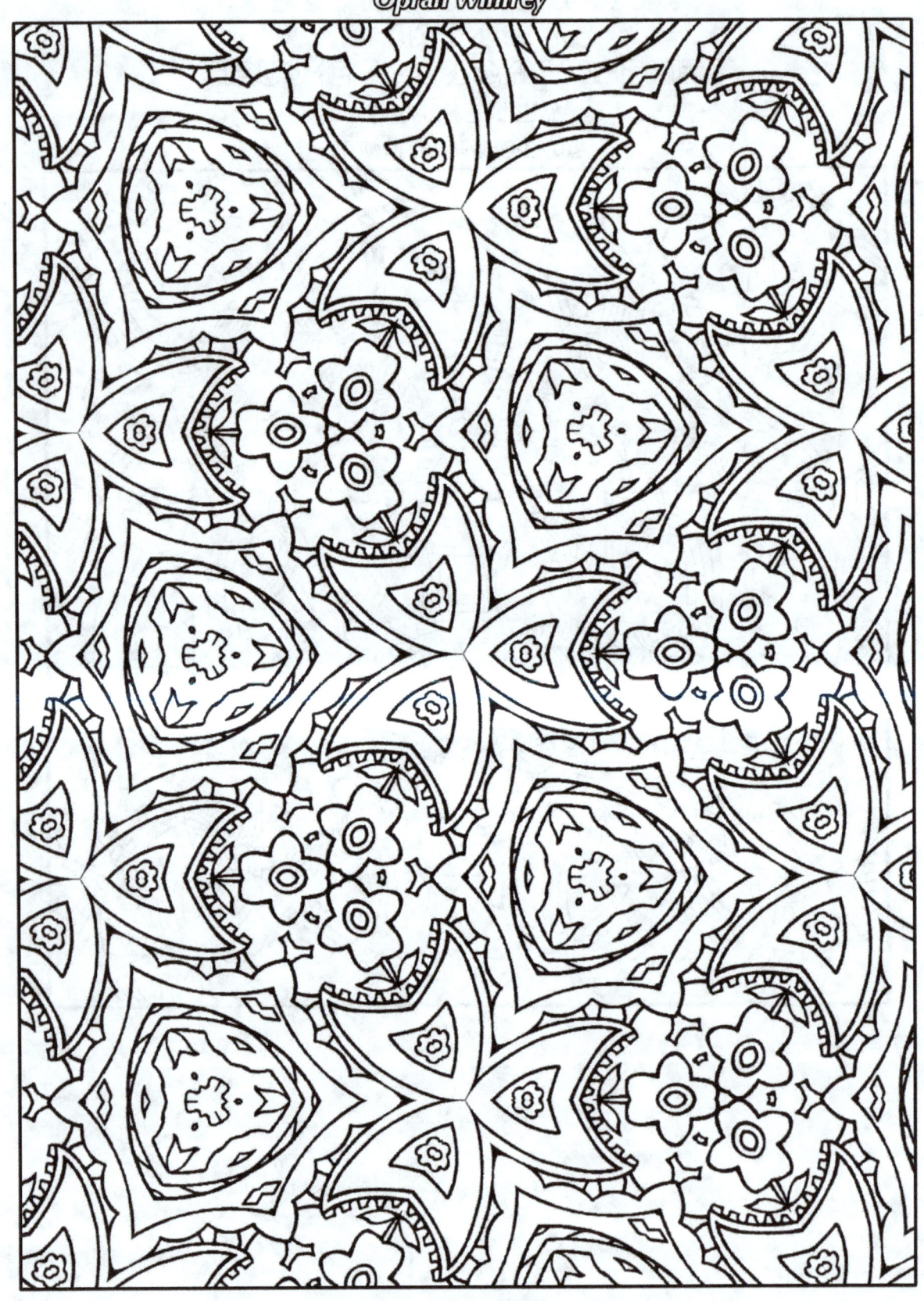

TOO MANY OF US ARE NOT LIVING OUR DREAMS BECAUSE WE ARE LIVING OUR FEARS.

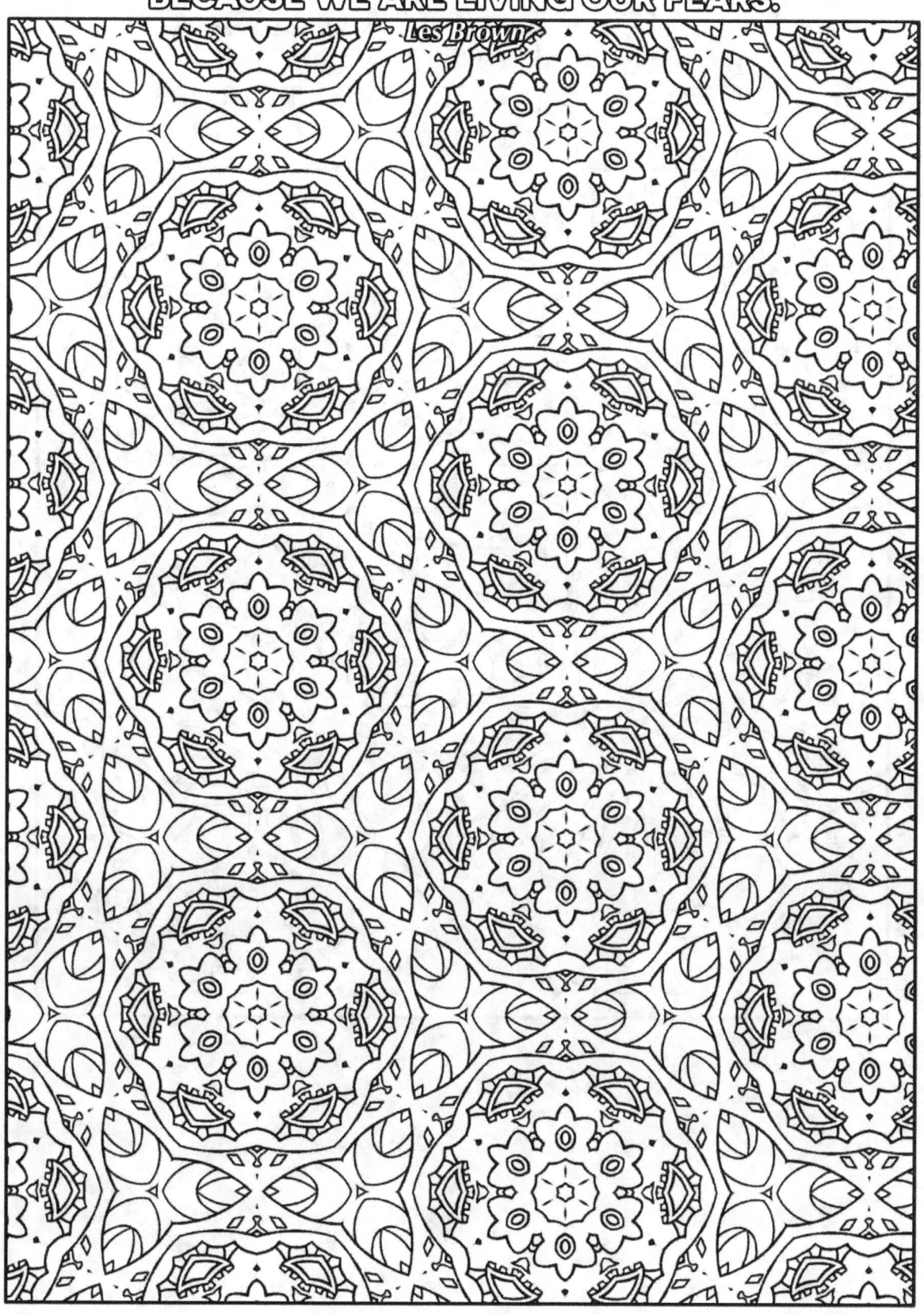

LIMITATIONS LIVE ONLY IN OUR MINDS.
BUT IF WE USE OUR IMAGINATIONS,
OUR POSSIBILITIES BECOME LIMITLESS.
Jamie Paolinetti

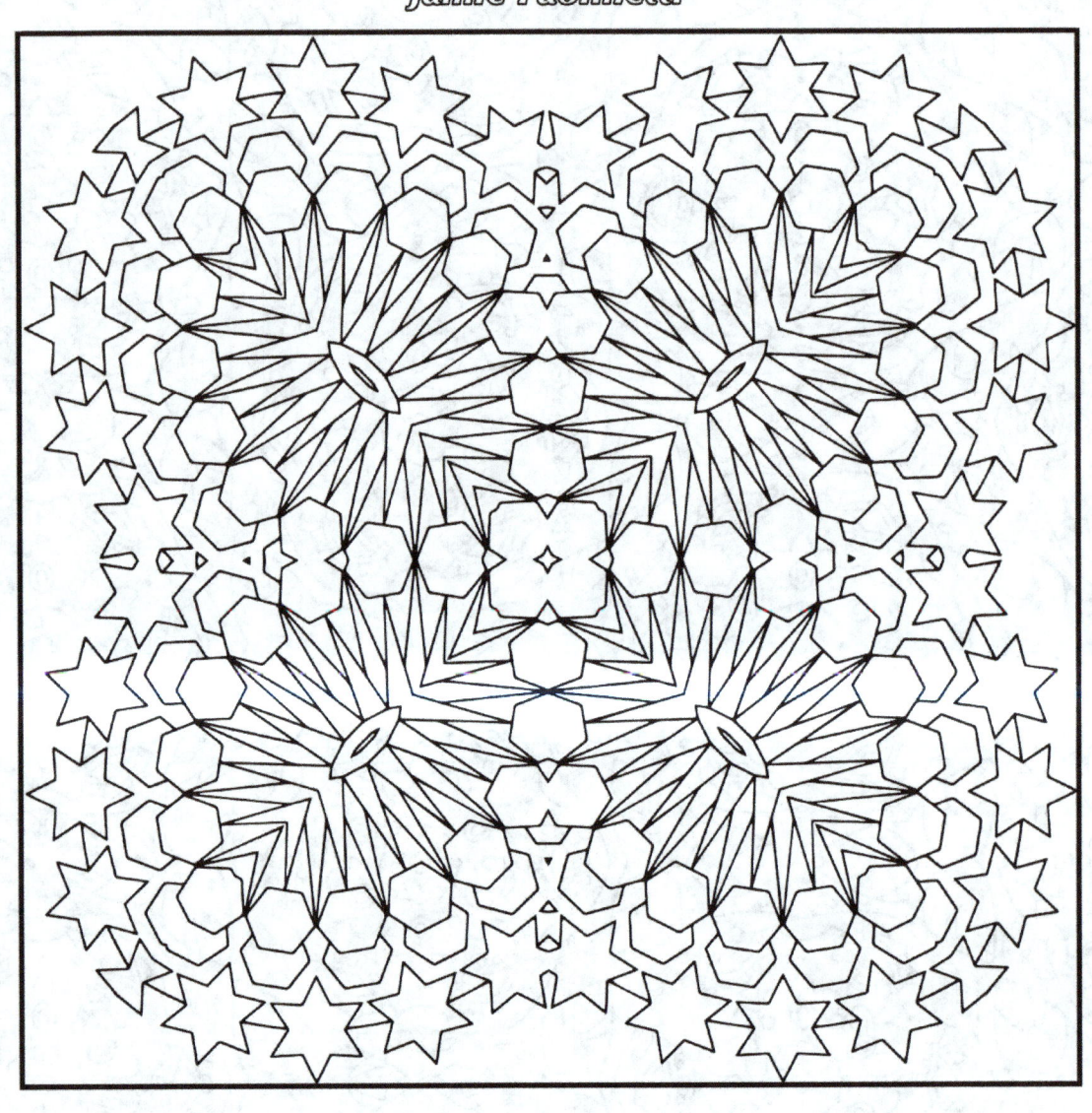

IT'S YOUR PLACE IN THE WORLD;
IT'S YOUR LIFE.
GO ON AND DO ALL YOU CAN WITH IT,
AND MAKE IT THE LIFE YOU WANT TO LIVE.
Mae Jemison

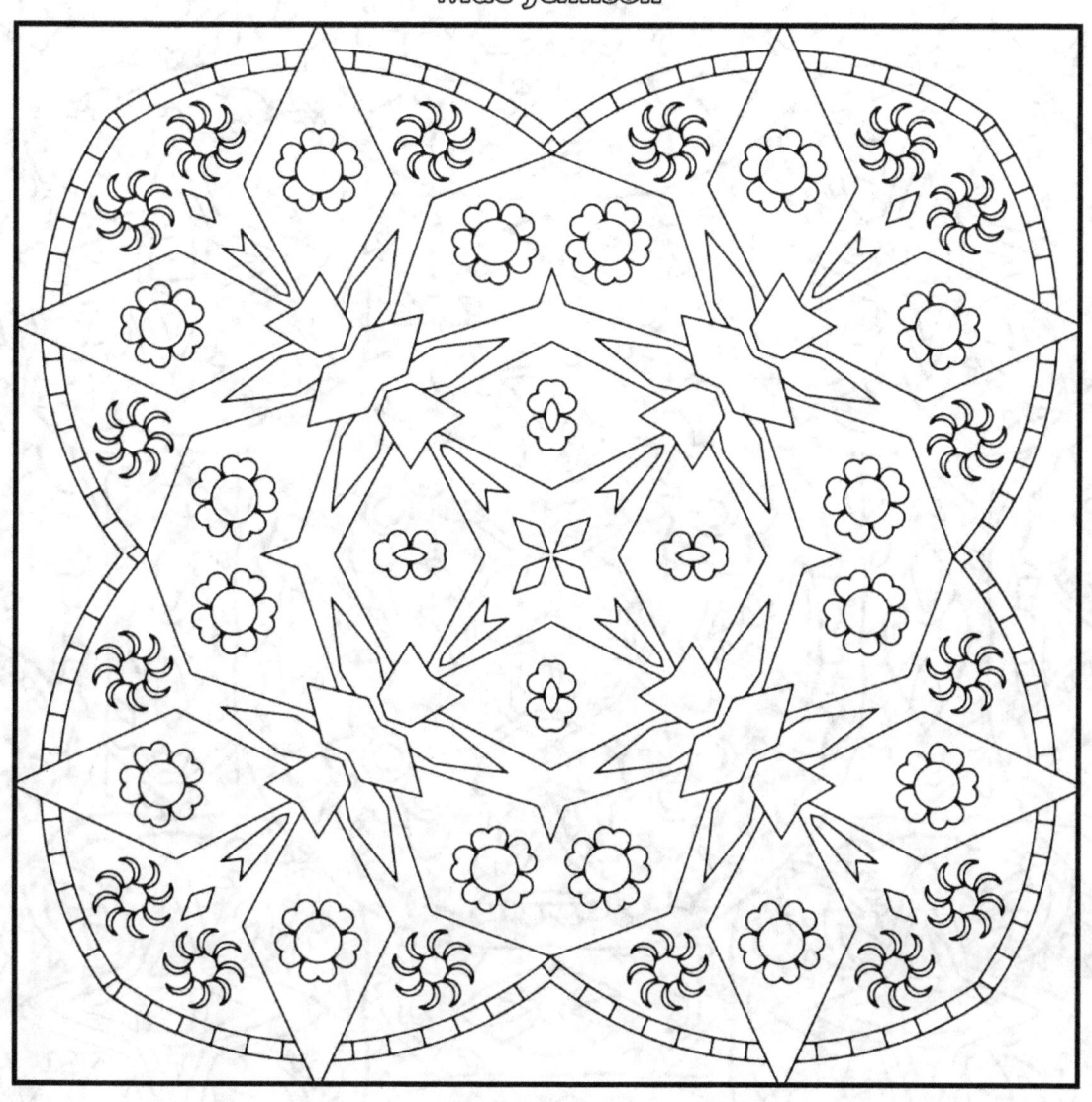

Farrah Gray

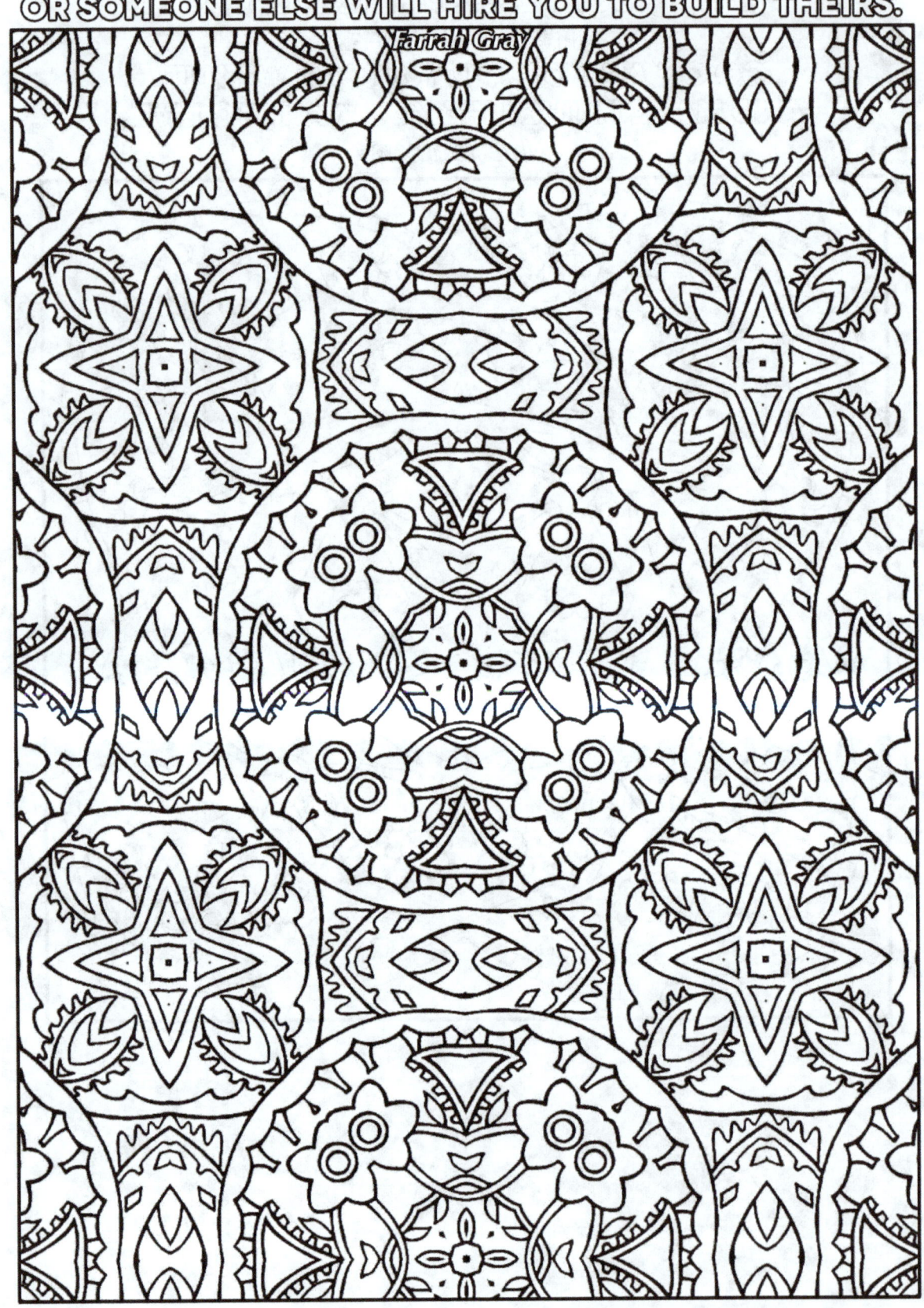

26

DREAM BIG AND DARE TO FAIL.
Norman Vaughan

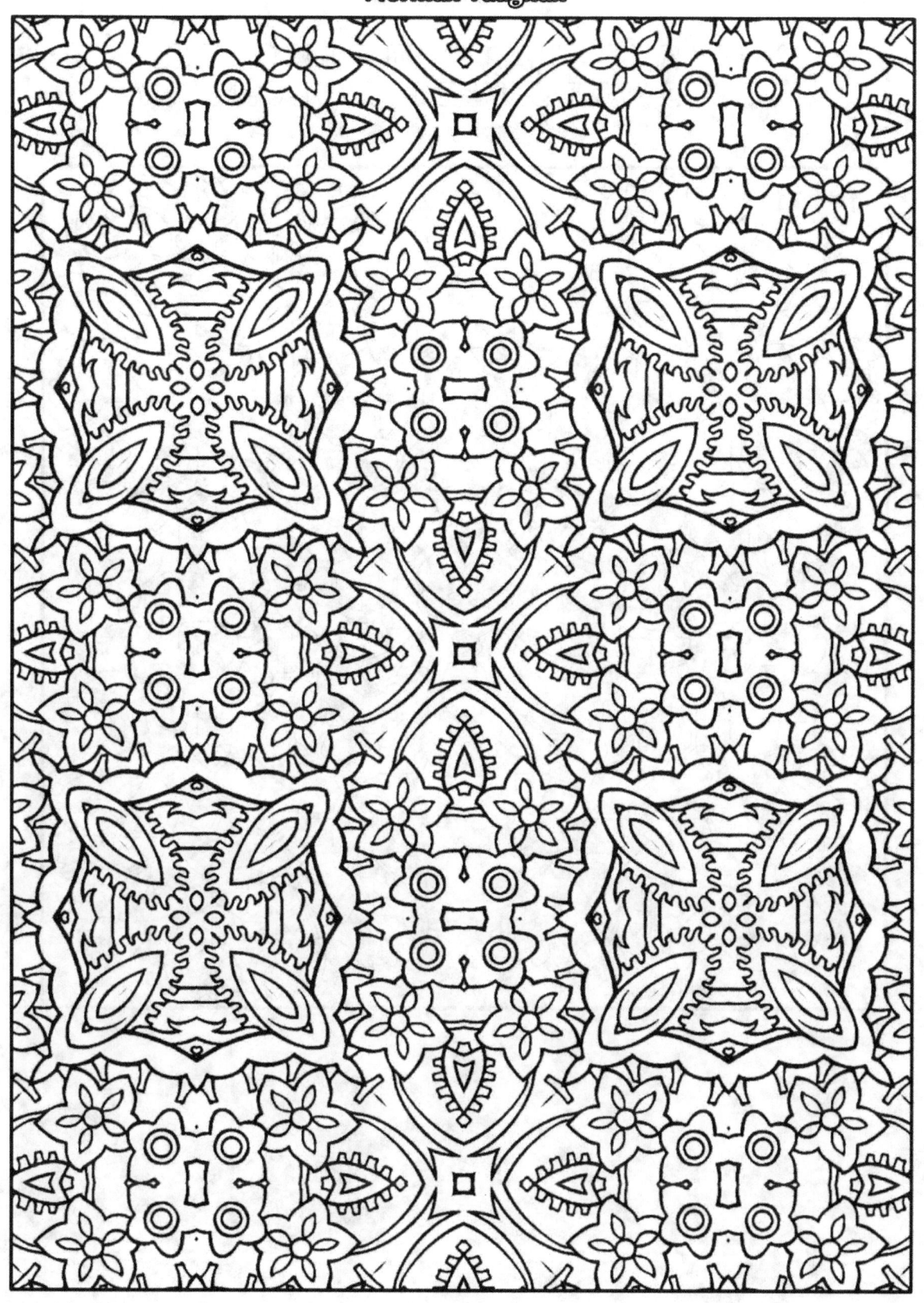

**YOU MAY BE DISAPPOINTED IF YOU FAIL,
BUT YOU ARE DOOMED IF YOU DON'T TRY.**
Beverly Sills

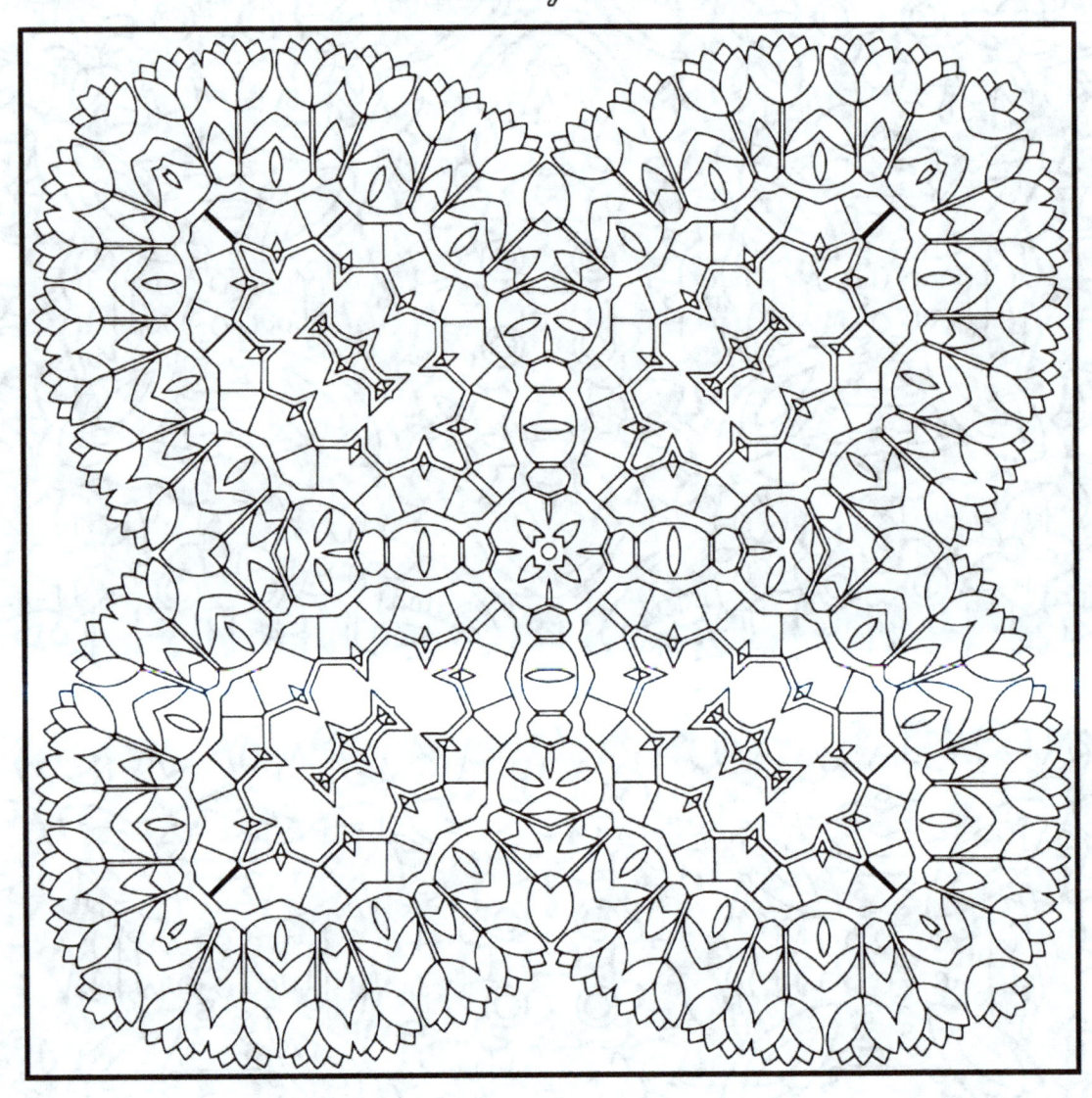

FIRST, HAVE A DEFINITE, CLEAR PRACTICAL IDEAL;
A GOAL, AN OBJECTIVE.
SECOND, HAVE THE NECESSARY MEANS
TO ACHIEVE YOUR ENDS;
WISDOM, MONEY, MATERIALS, AND METHODS.
THIRD, ADJUST ALL YOUR MEANS TO THAT END.

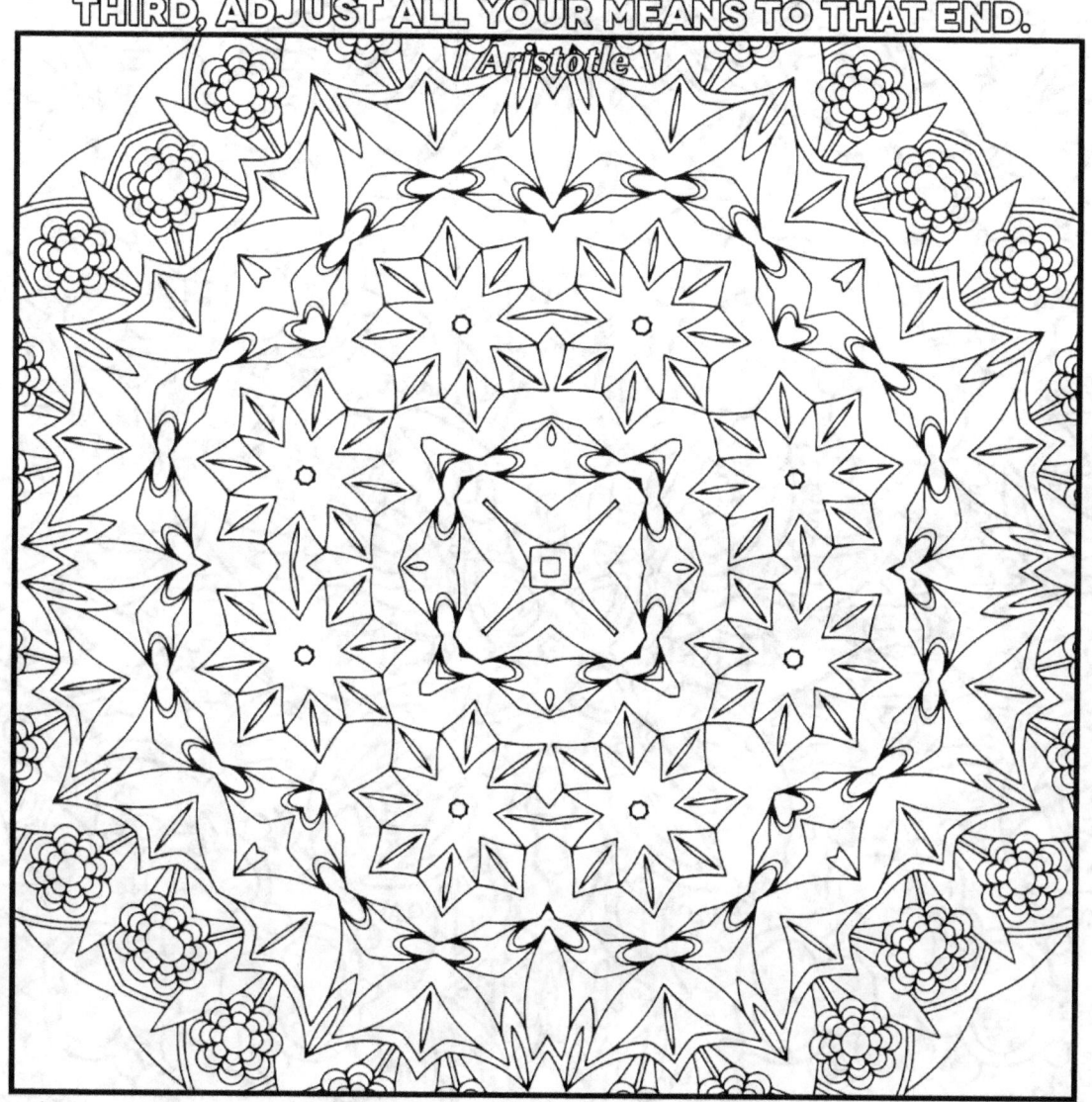

Aristotle

FALL SEVEN TIMES AND STAND UP EIGHT.
Japanese Proverb

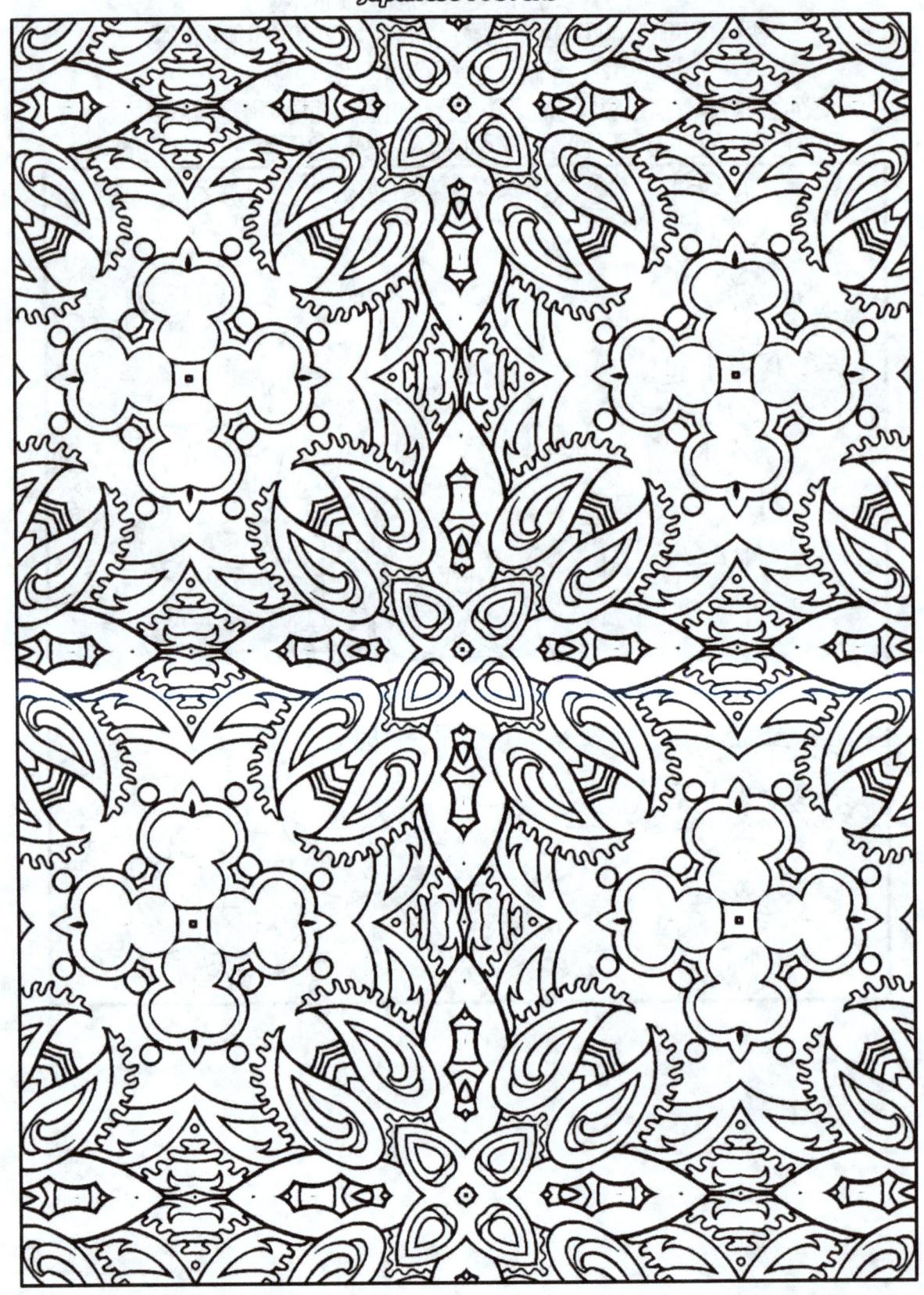

THE BEST REVENGE IS MASSIVE SUCCESS.
Frank Sinatra

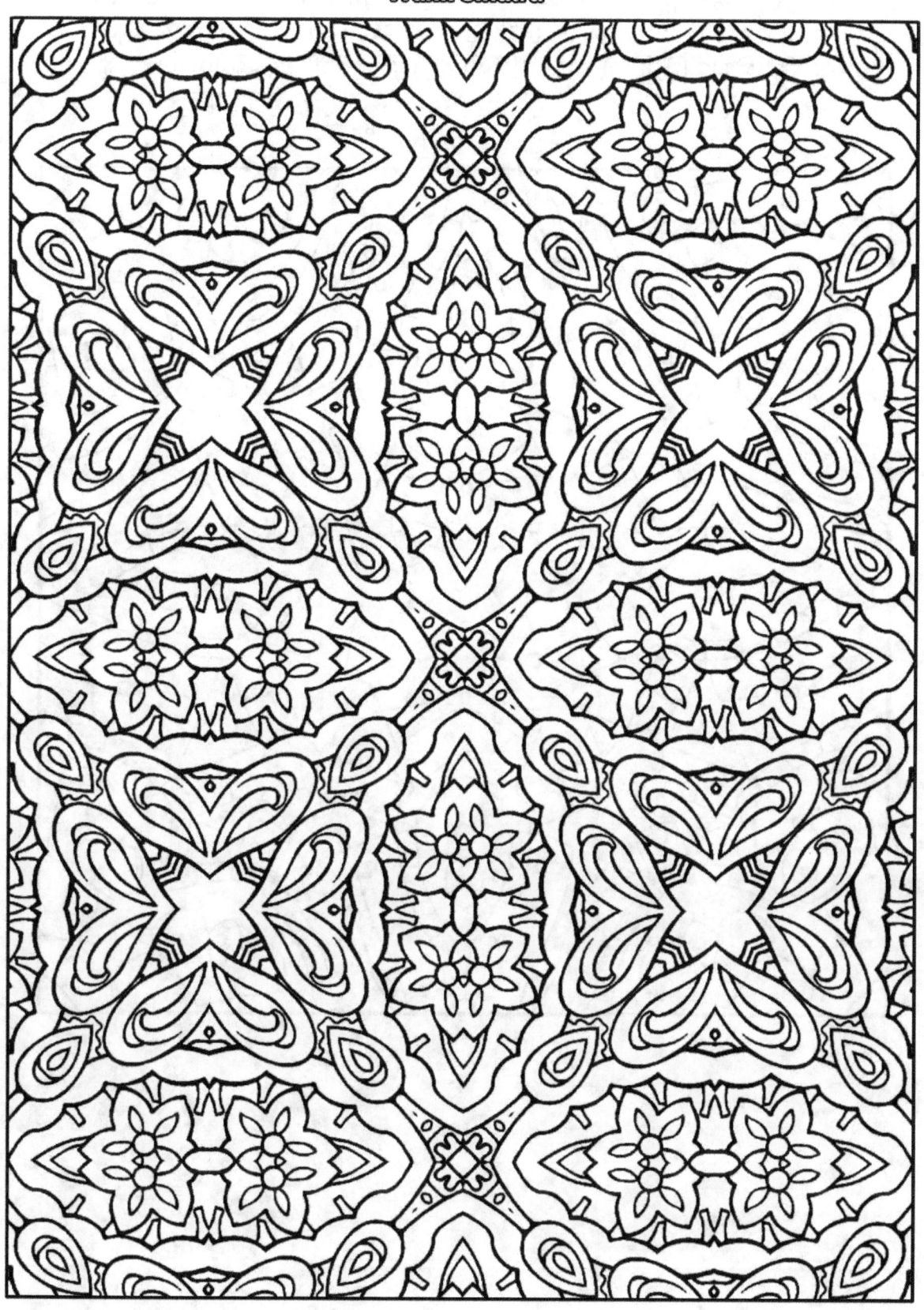

WHEN I STAND BEFORE GOD AT THE END OF MY LIFE,
I WOULD HOPE THAT I WOULD NOT HAVE
A SINGLE BIT OF TALENT LEFT AND COULD SAY,
I USED EVERYTHING YOU GAVE ME.
Erma Bombeck

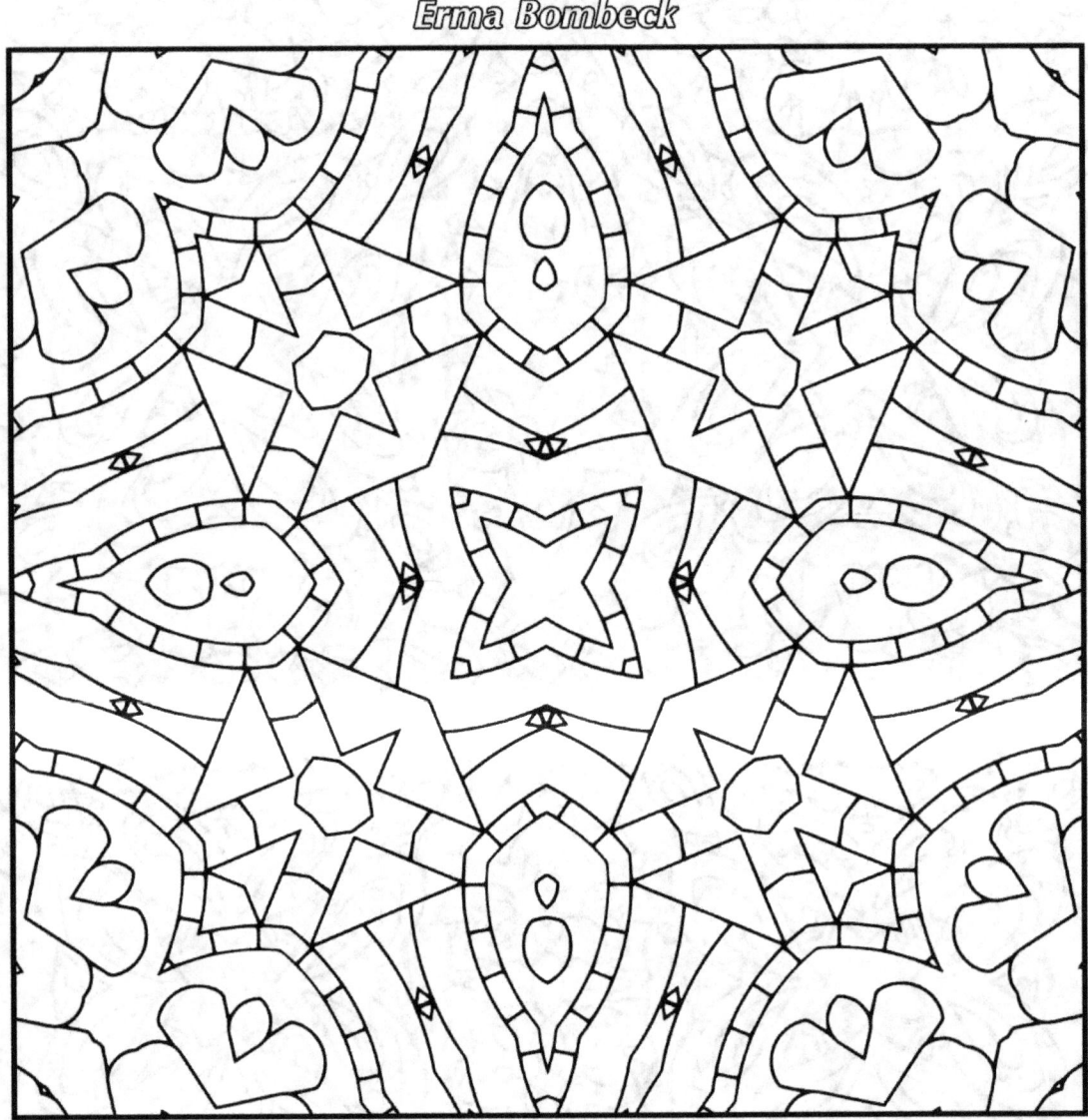

I'VE MISSED MORE THAN 9000 SHOTS IN MY CAREER.
I'VE LOST ALMOST 300 GAMES.
26 TIMES I'VE BEEN TRUSTED TO TAKE
THE GAME WINNING SHOT AND MISSED.
I'VE FAILED OVER AND OVER AND OVER AGAIN
IN MY LIFE. AND THAT IS WHY I SUCCEED.

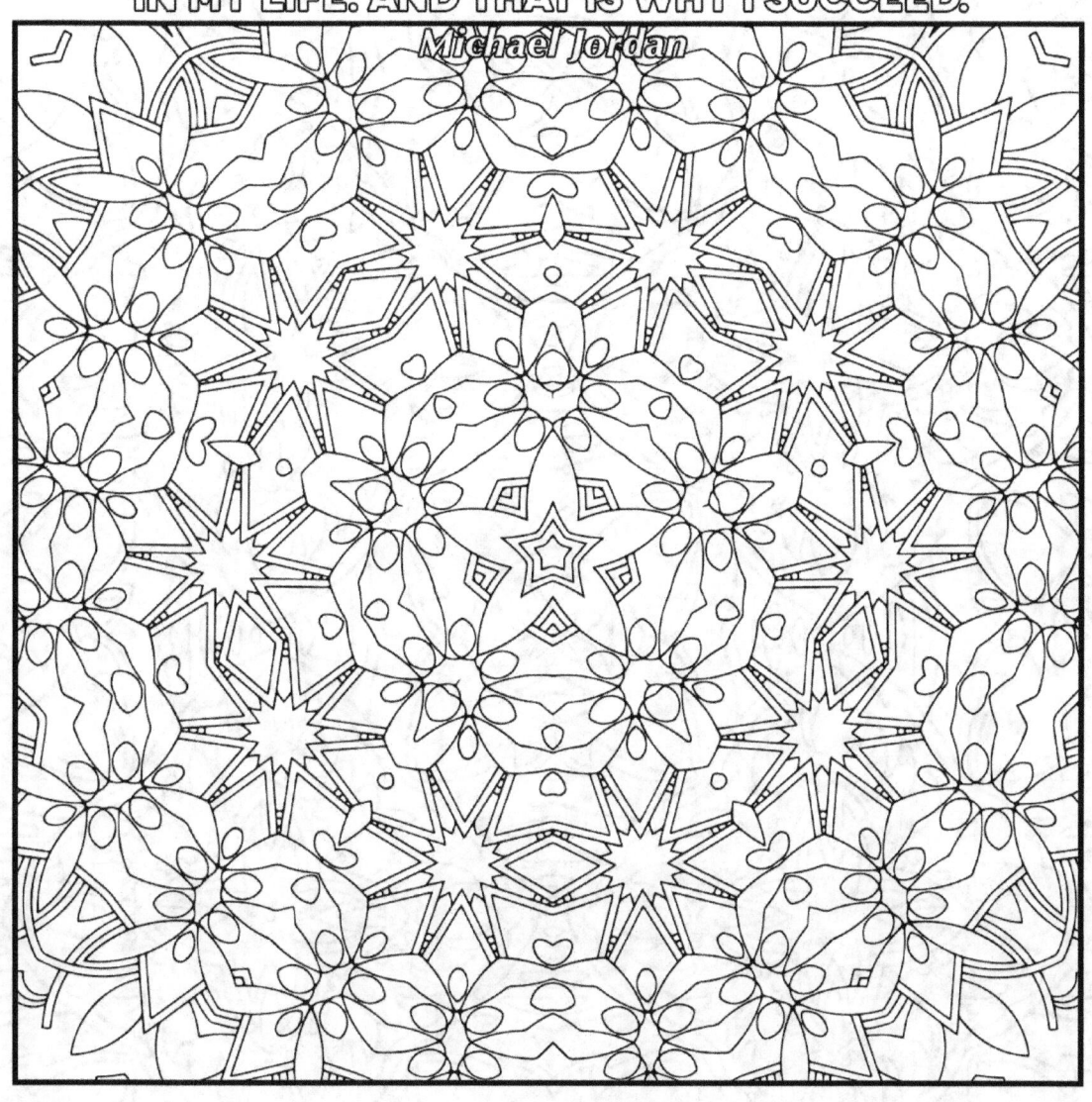

Michael Jordan

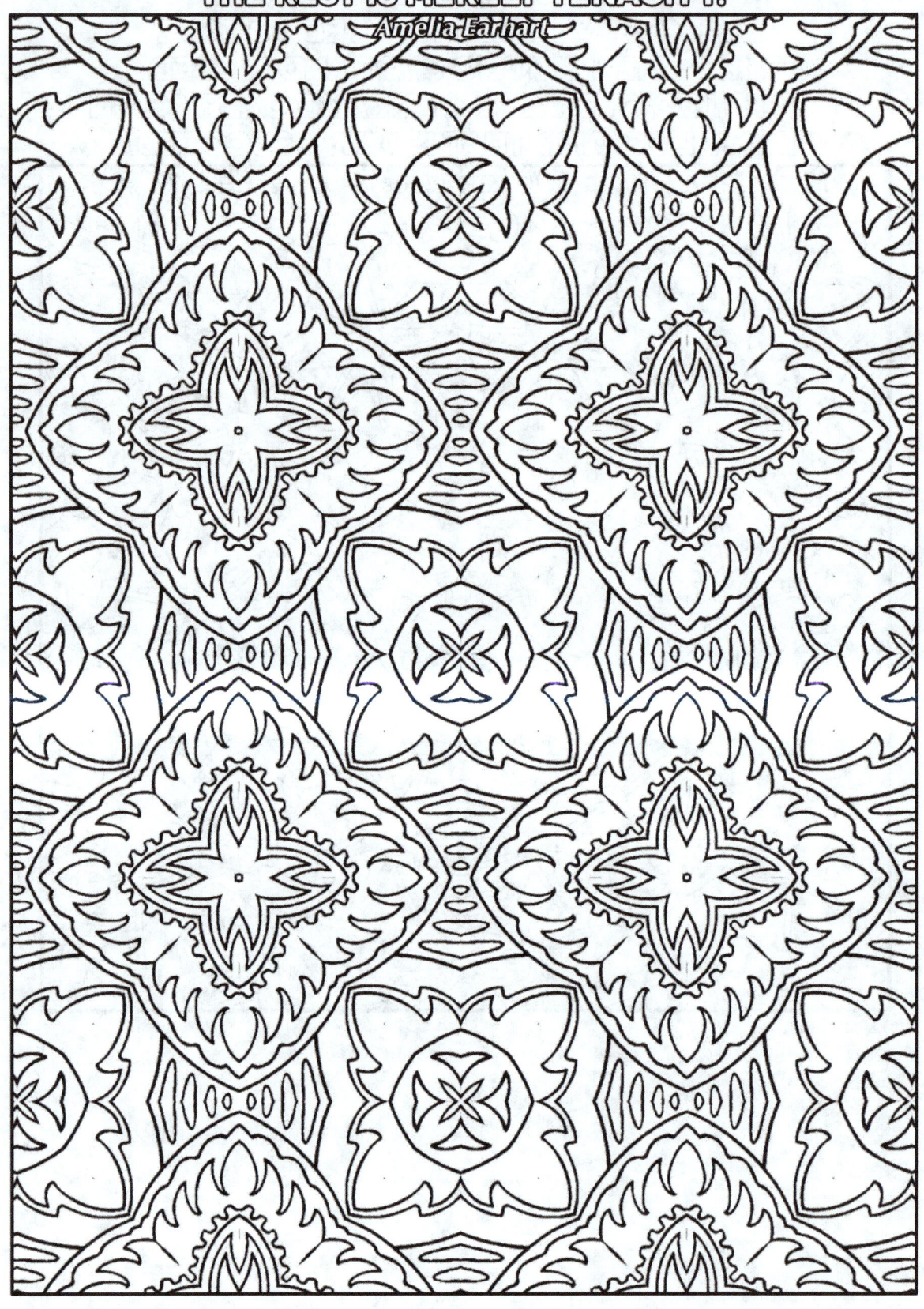

34

I ATTRIBUTE MY SUCCESS TO THIS:
I NEVER GAVE OR TOOK ANY EXCUSE.
Florence Nightingale

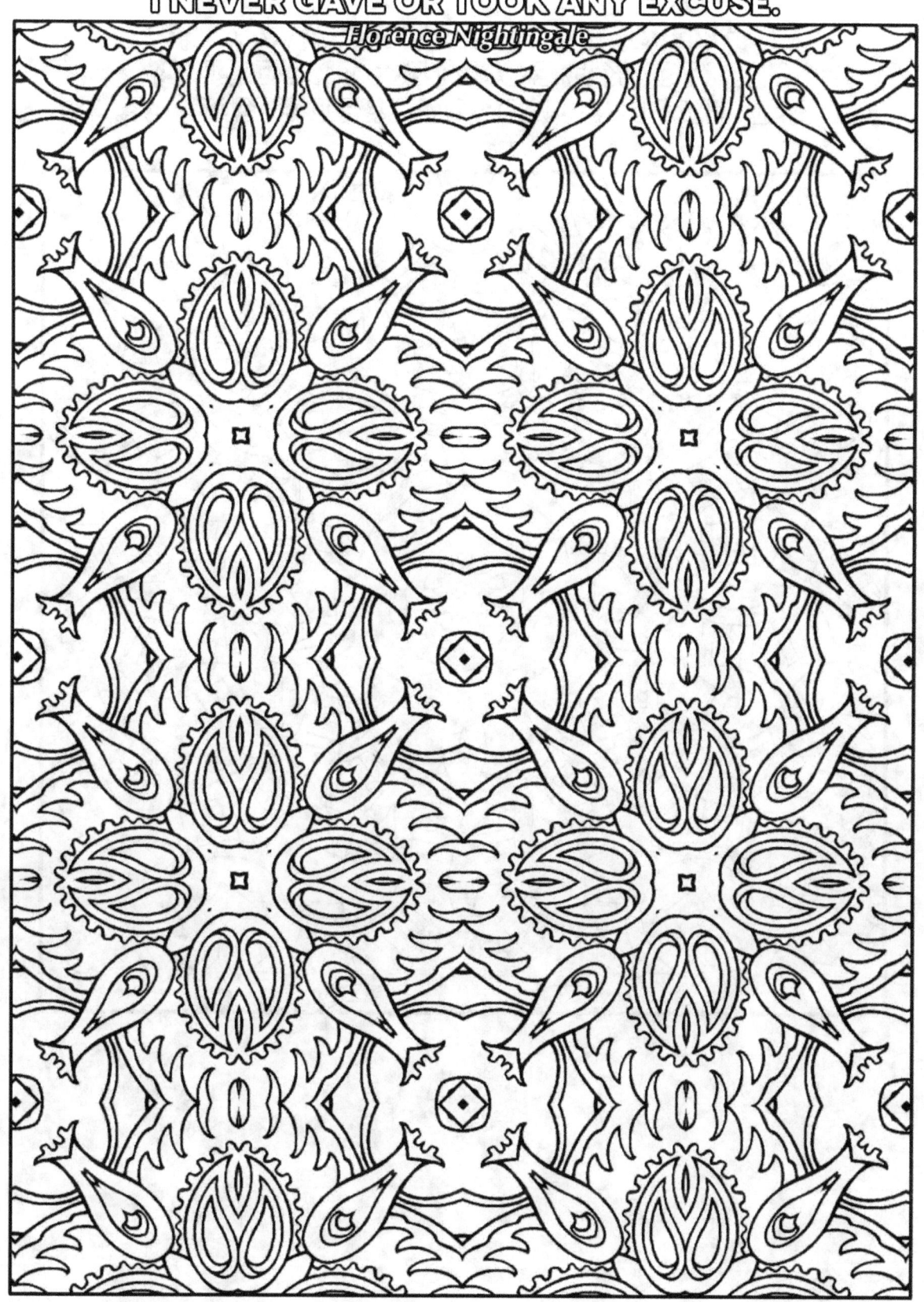

TWO ROADS DIVERGED IN A WOOD,
AND I TOOK THE ONE LESS TRAVELED BY,
AND THAT HAS MADE ALL THE DIFFERENCE.
Robert Frost

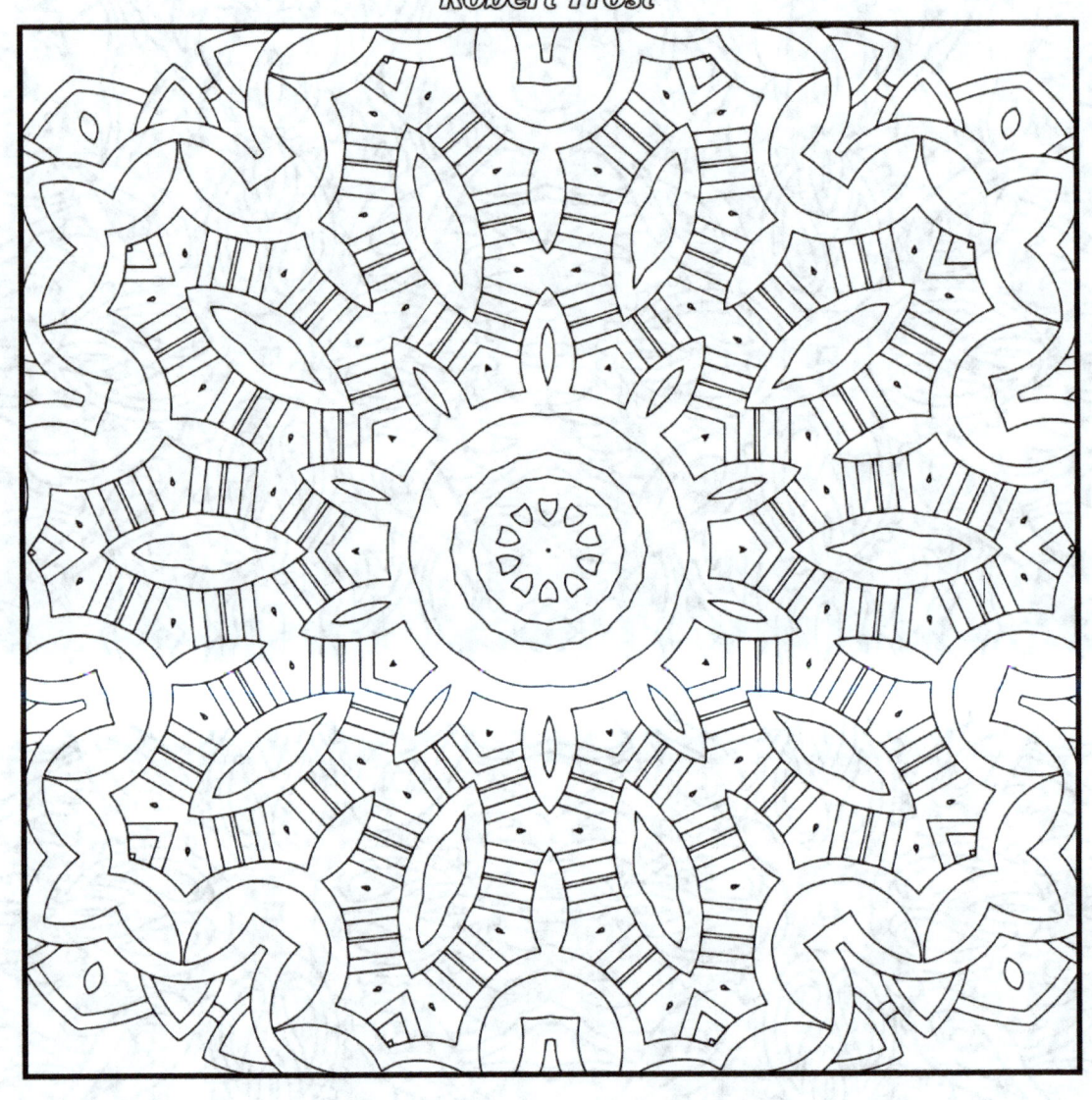

IF YOU HEAR A VOICE WITHIN YOU SAY
"YOU CANNOT PAINT," THEN BY ALL MEANS PAINT
AND THAT VOICE WILL BE SILENCED.
Vincent Van Gogh

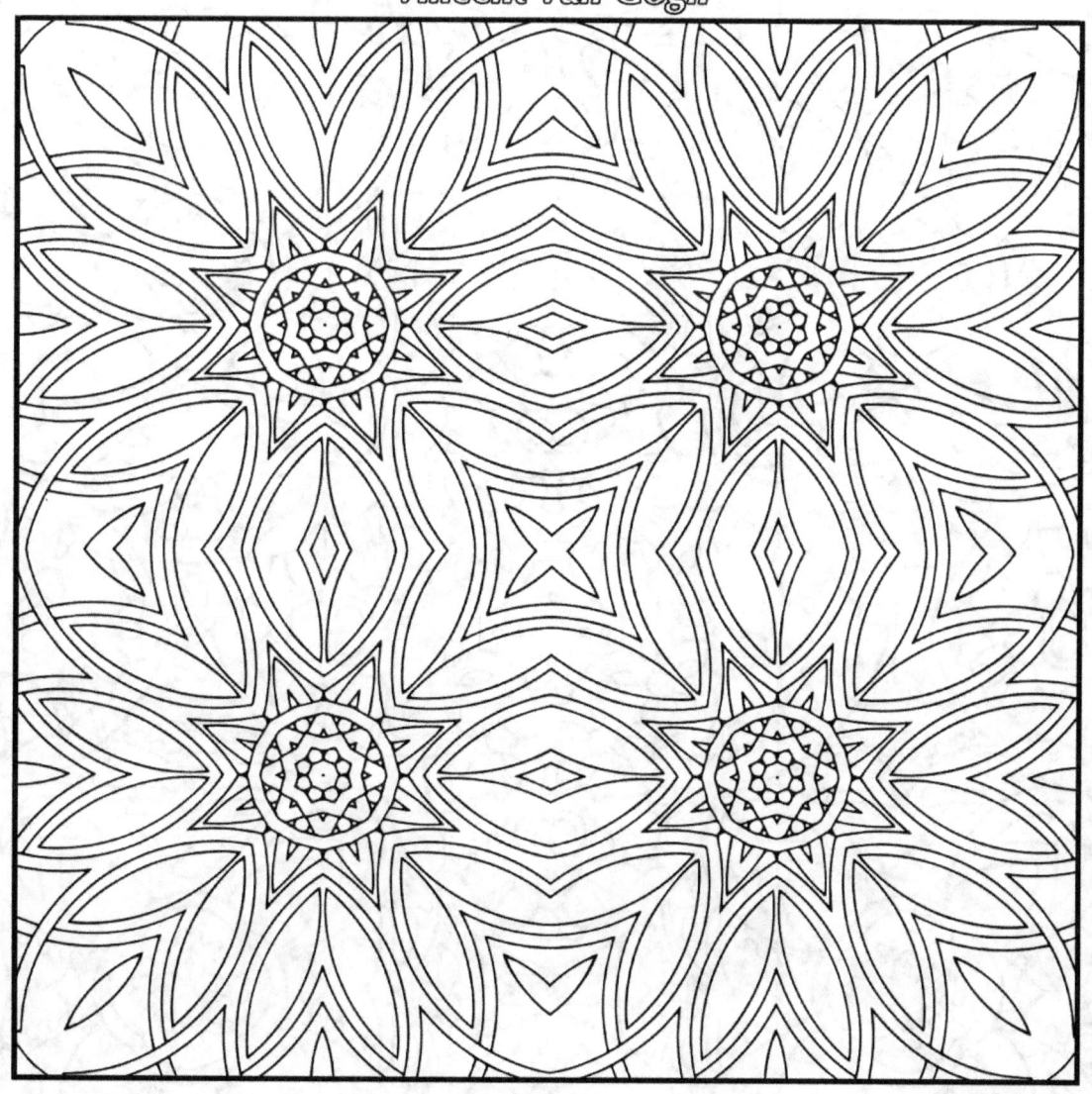

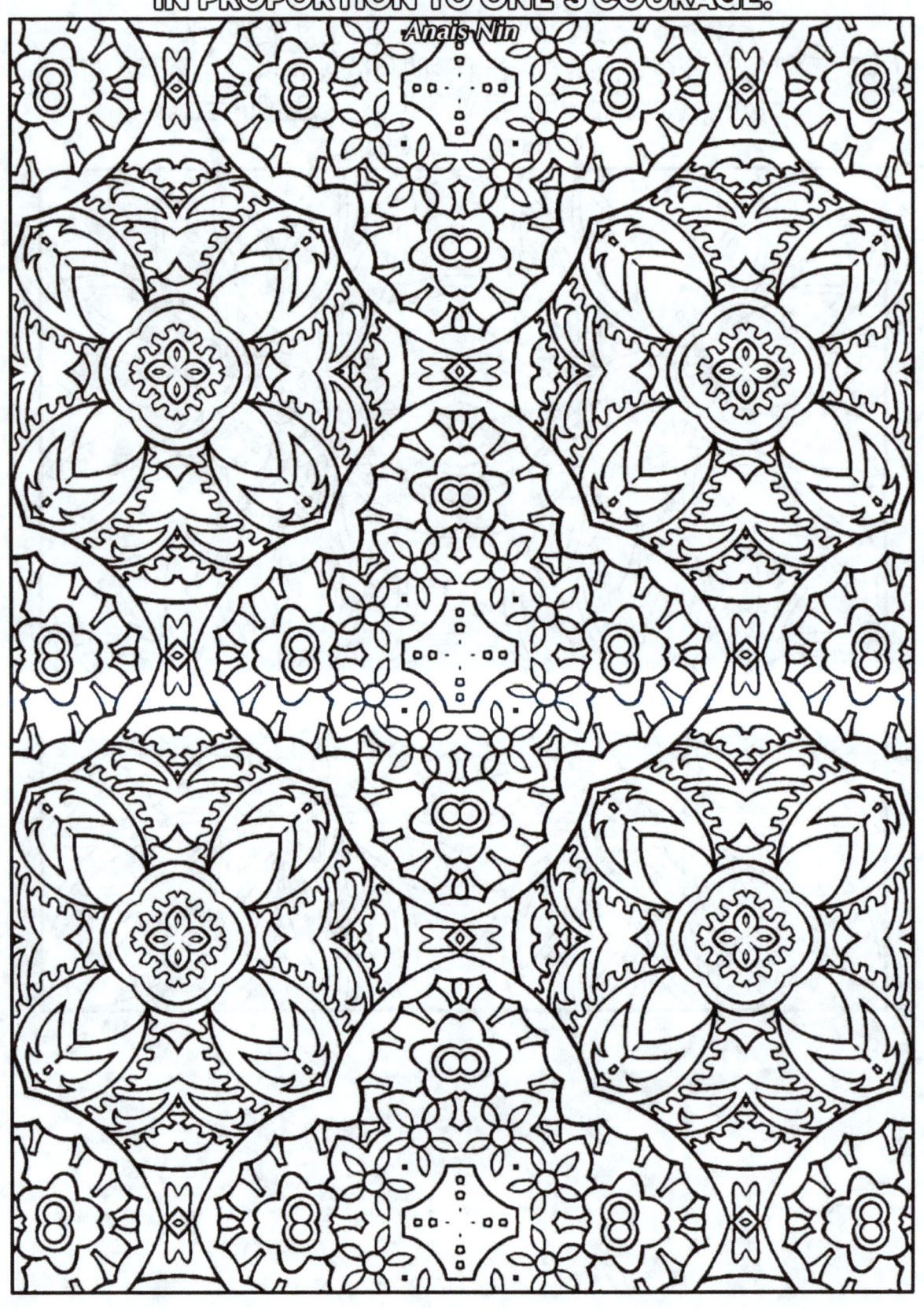

EITHER YOU RUN THE DAY, OR THE DAY RUNS YOU.
Jim Rohn

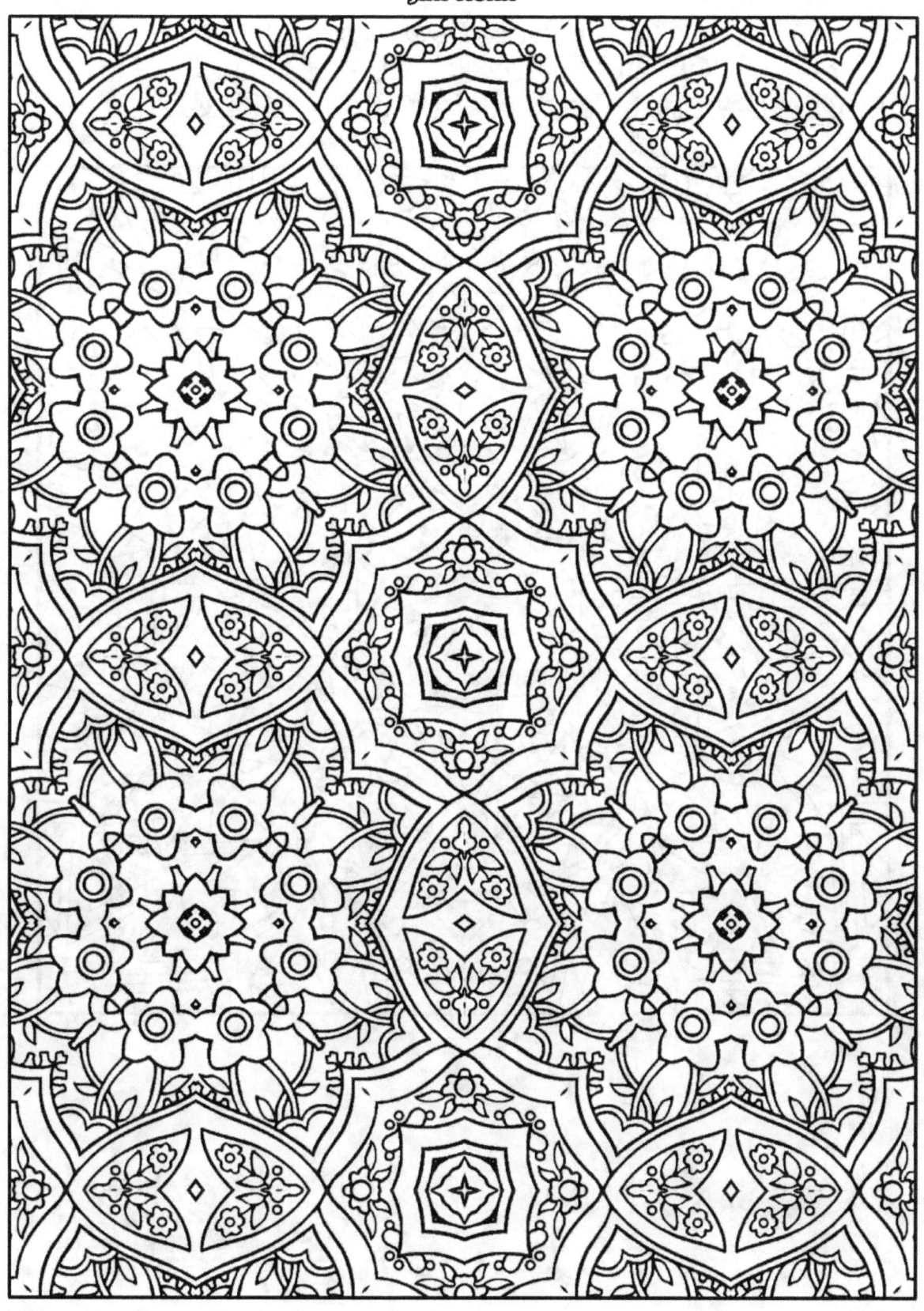

**WHATEVER YOU CAN DO,
OR DREAM YOU CAN, BEGIN IT.
BOLDNESS HAS GENIUS, POWER AND MAGIC IN IT.**
Johann Wolfgang von Goethe

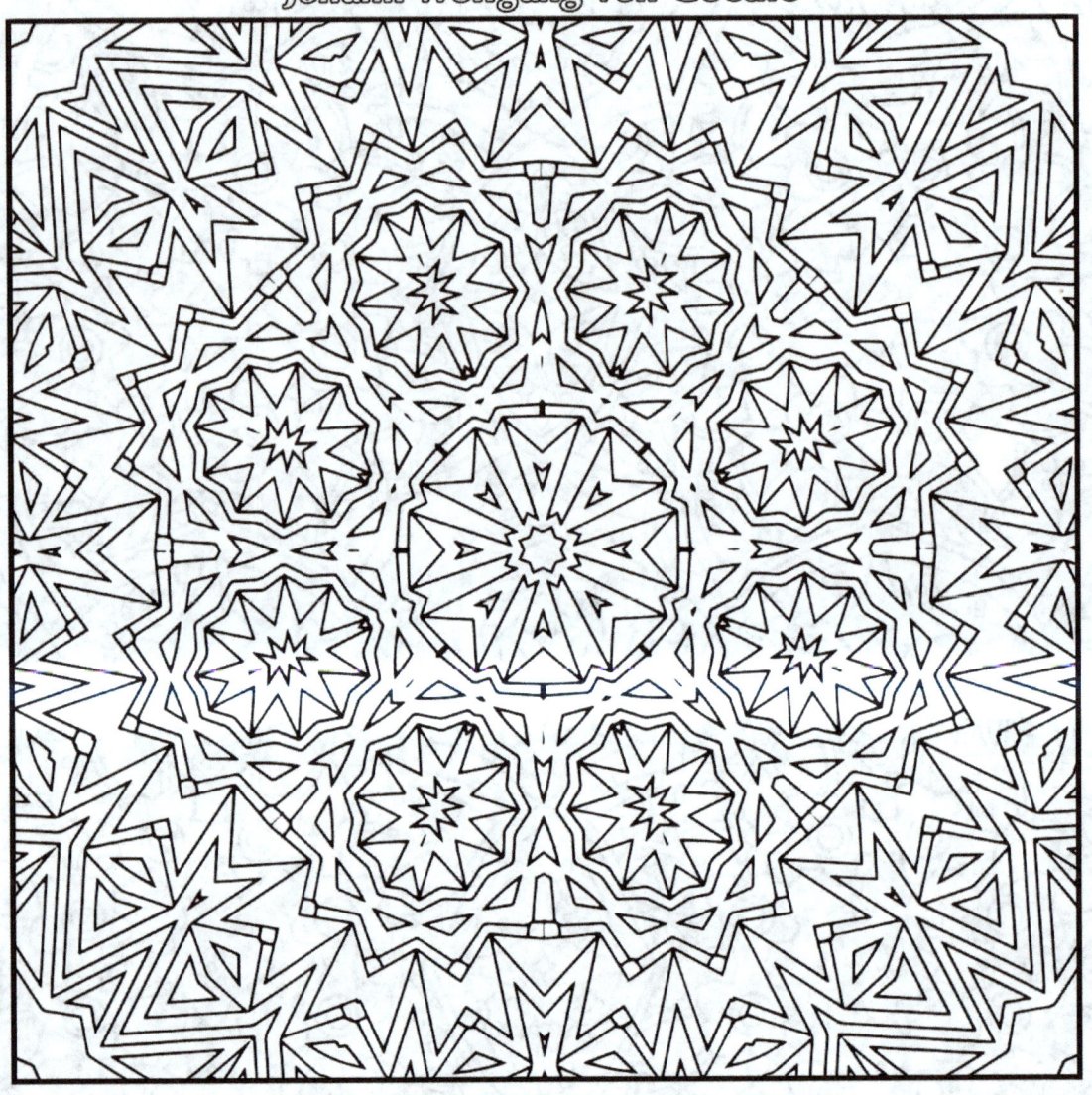

**IF YOU WANT YOUR CHILDREN TO TURN OUT WELL,
SPEND TWICE AS MUCH TIME WITH THEM,
AND HALF AS MUCH MONEY.**
Abigail Van Buren

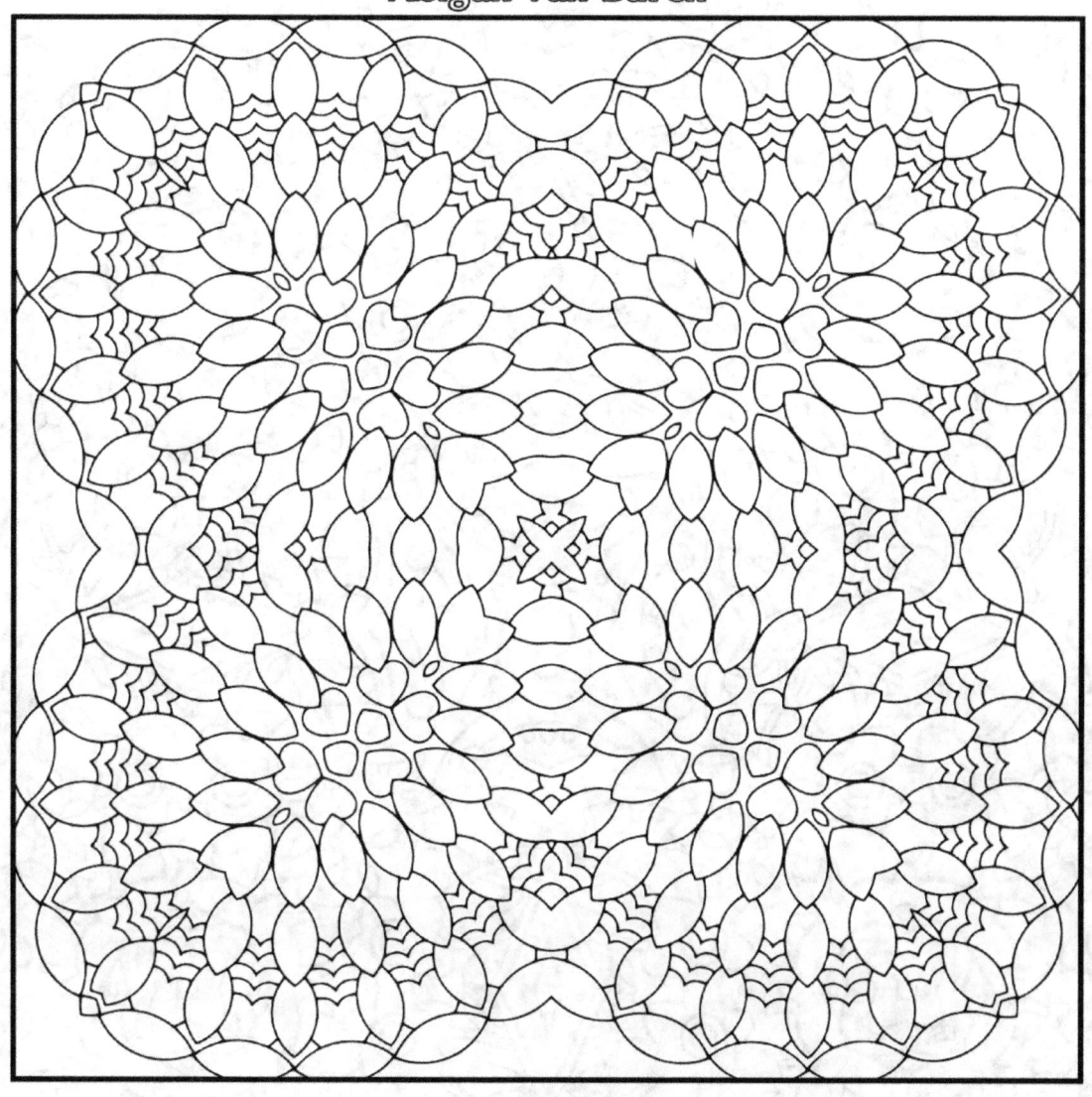

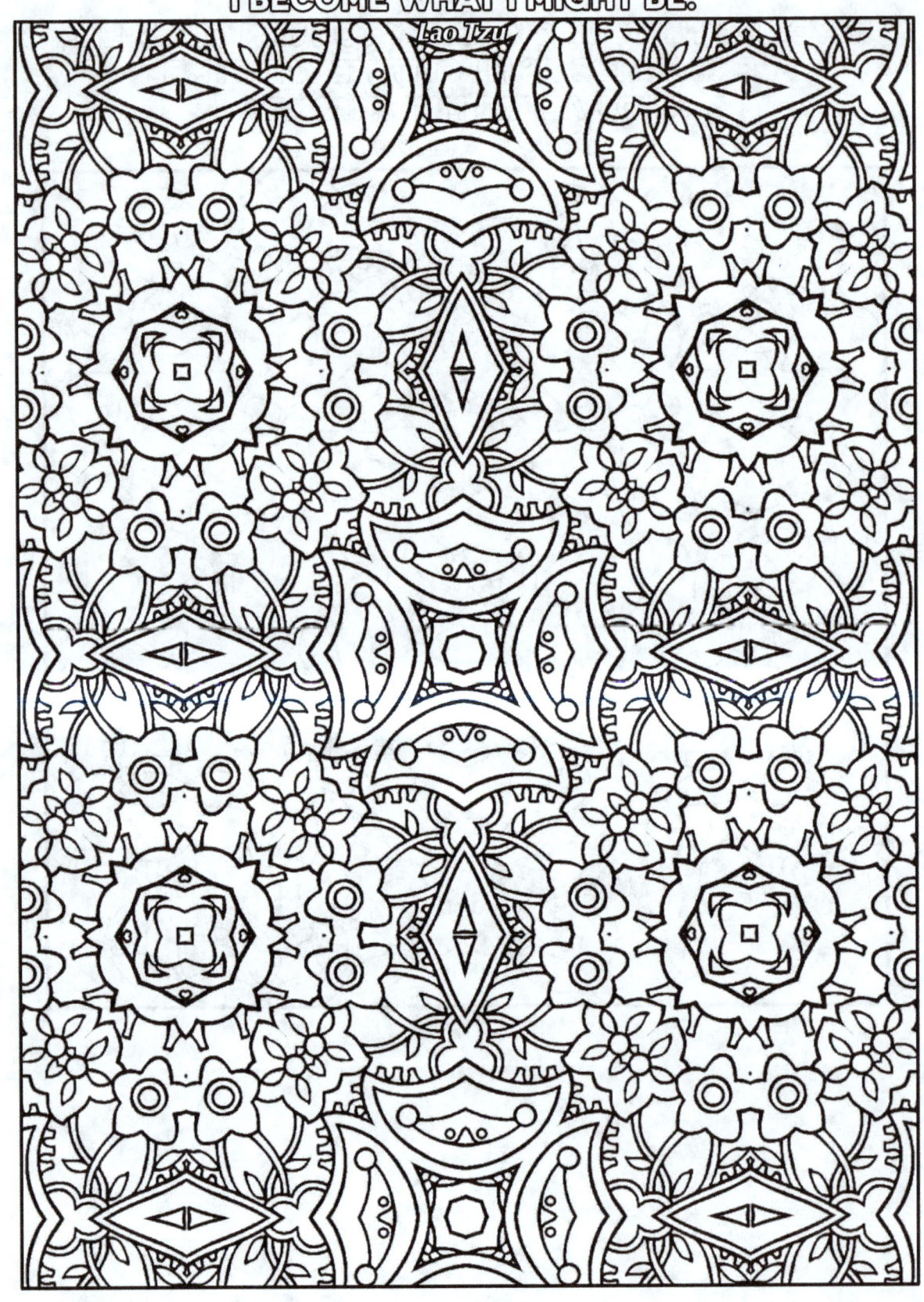

DREAMING, AFTER ALL, IS A FORM OF PLANNING.
Gloria Steinem

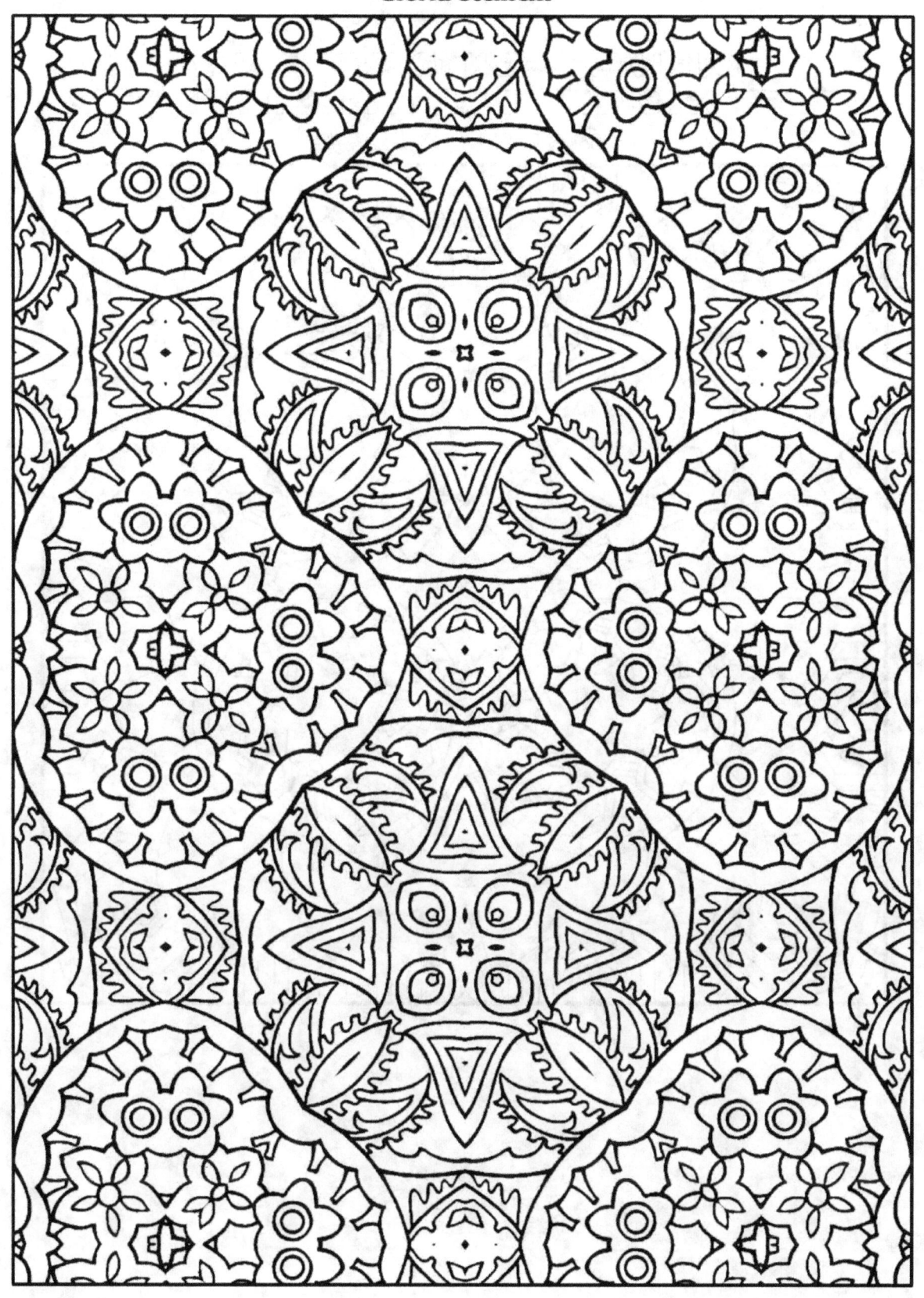

**OUR LIVES BEGIN TO END THE DAY
WE BECOME SILENT ABOUT THINGS THAT MATTER.**
Martin Luther King Jr.

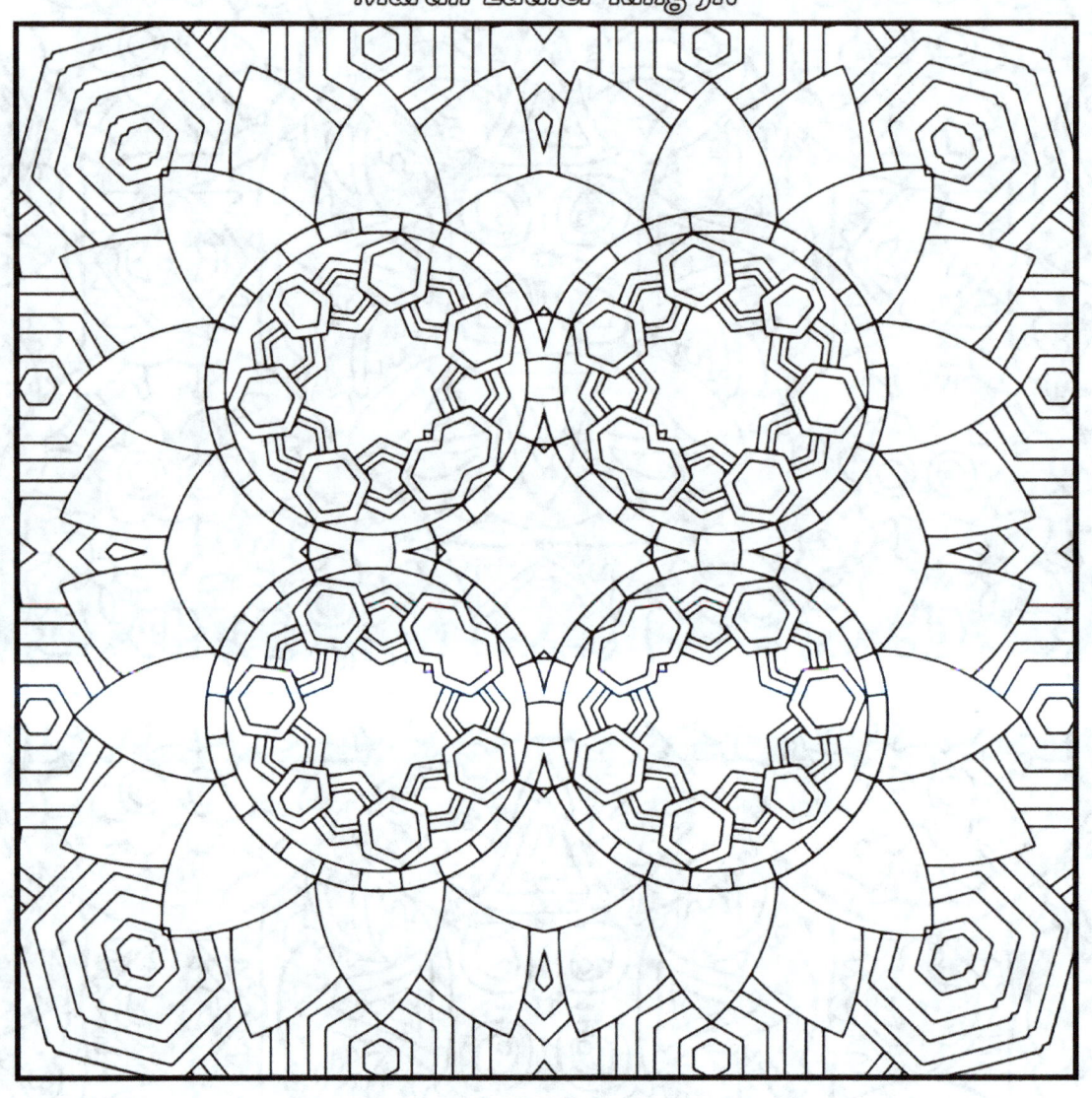

REMEMBER THAT NOT GETTING WHAT YOU WANT
IS SOMETIMES A WONDERFUL STROKE OF LUCK.
Dalai Lama

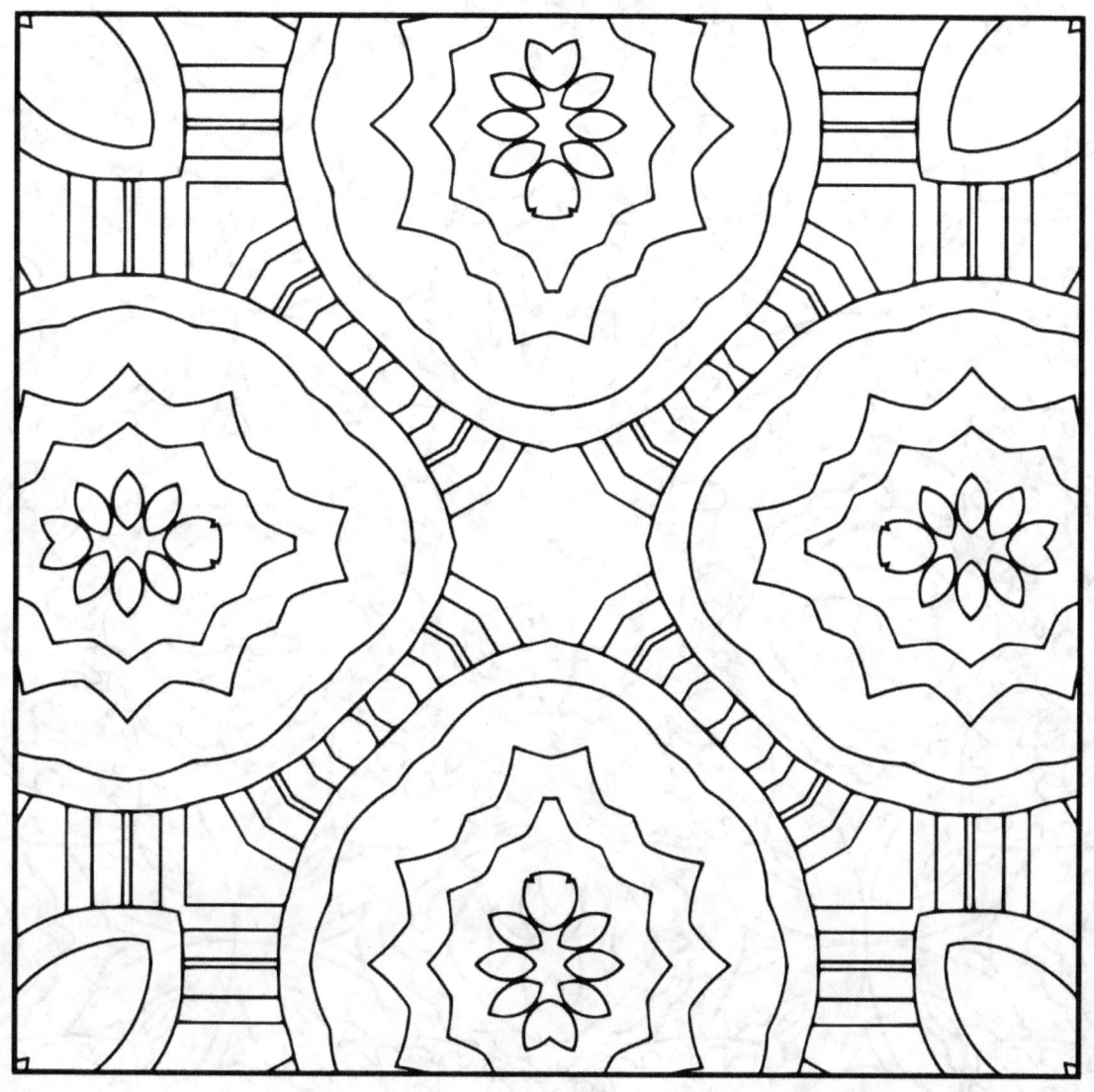

DO WHAT YOU CAN, WHERE YOU ARE, WITH WHAT YOU HAVE.

Teddy Roosevelt

IF YOU WANT TO LIFT YOURSELF UP, LIFT UP SOMEONE ELSE.

Booker T. Washington

WE MUST BELIEVE THAT WE ARE GIFTED
FOR SOMETHING,
AND THAT THIS THING,
AT WHATEVER COST, MUST BE ATTAINED.
Marie Curie

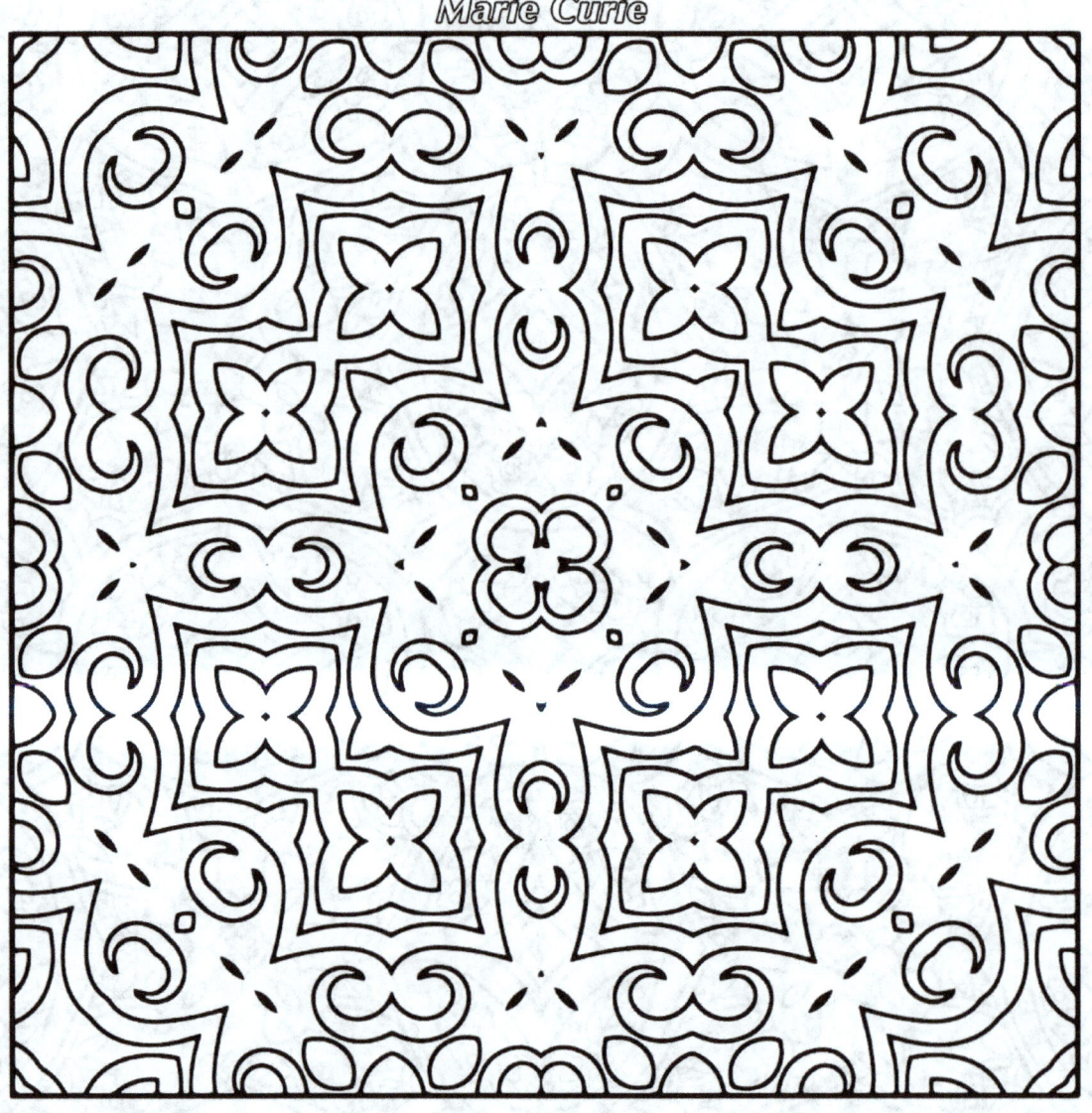

FEW THINGS CAN HELP AN INDIVIDUAL
MORE THAN TO PLACE RESPONSIBILITY ON HIM,
AND TO LET HIM KNOW THAT YOU TRUST HIM.
Booker T. Washington

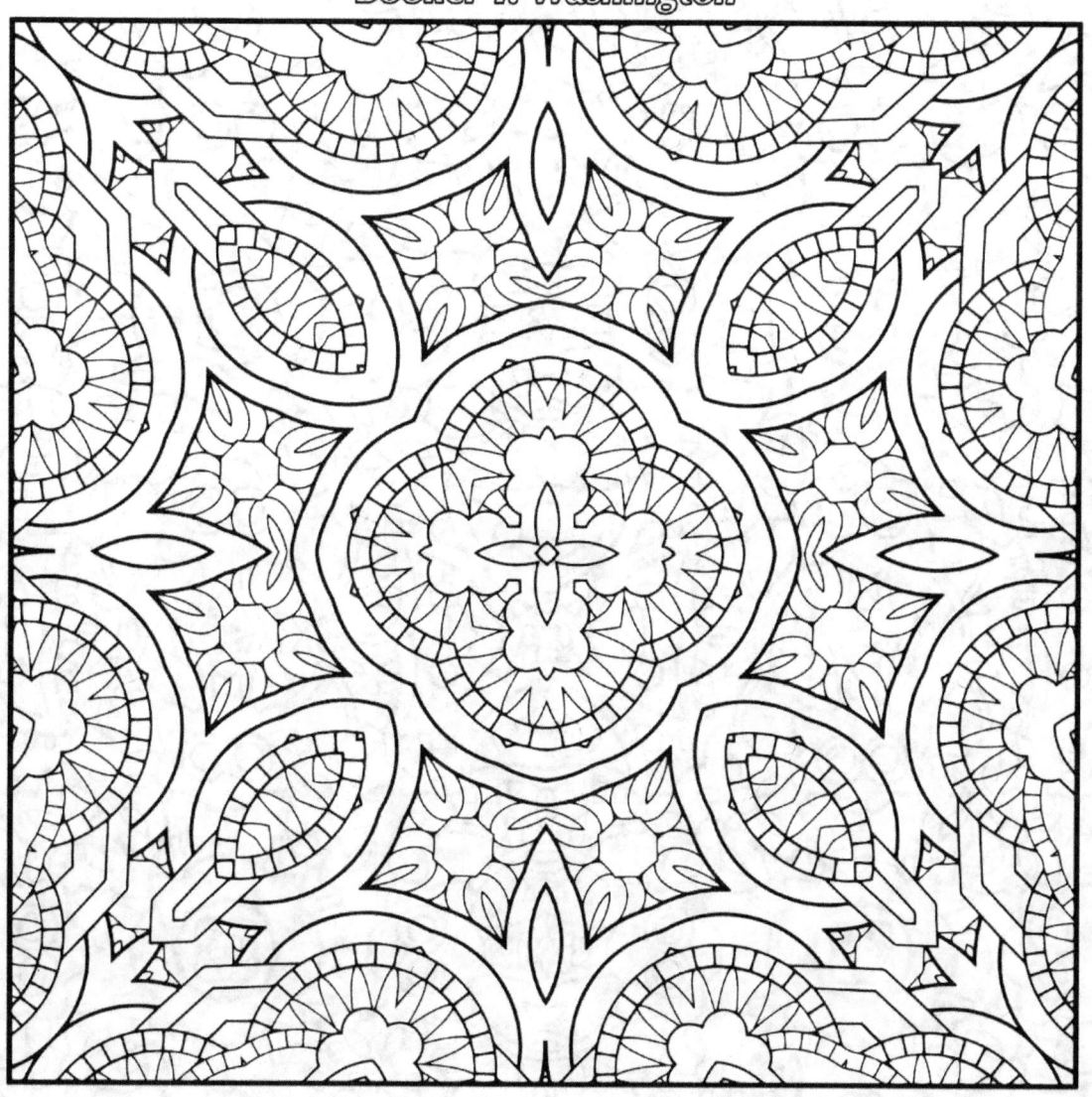

START WHERE YOU ARE. USE WHAT YOU HAVE. DO WHAT YOU CAN.

Arthur Ashe

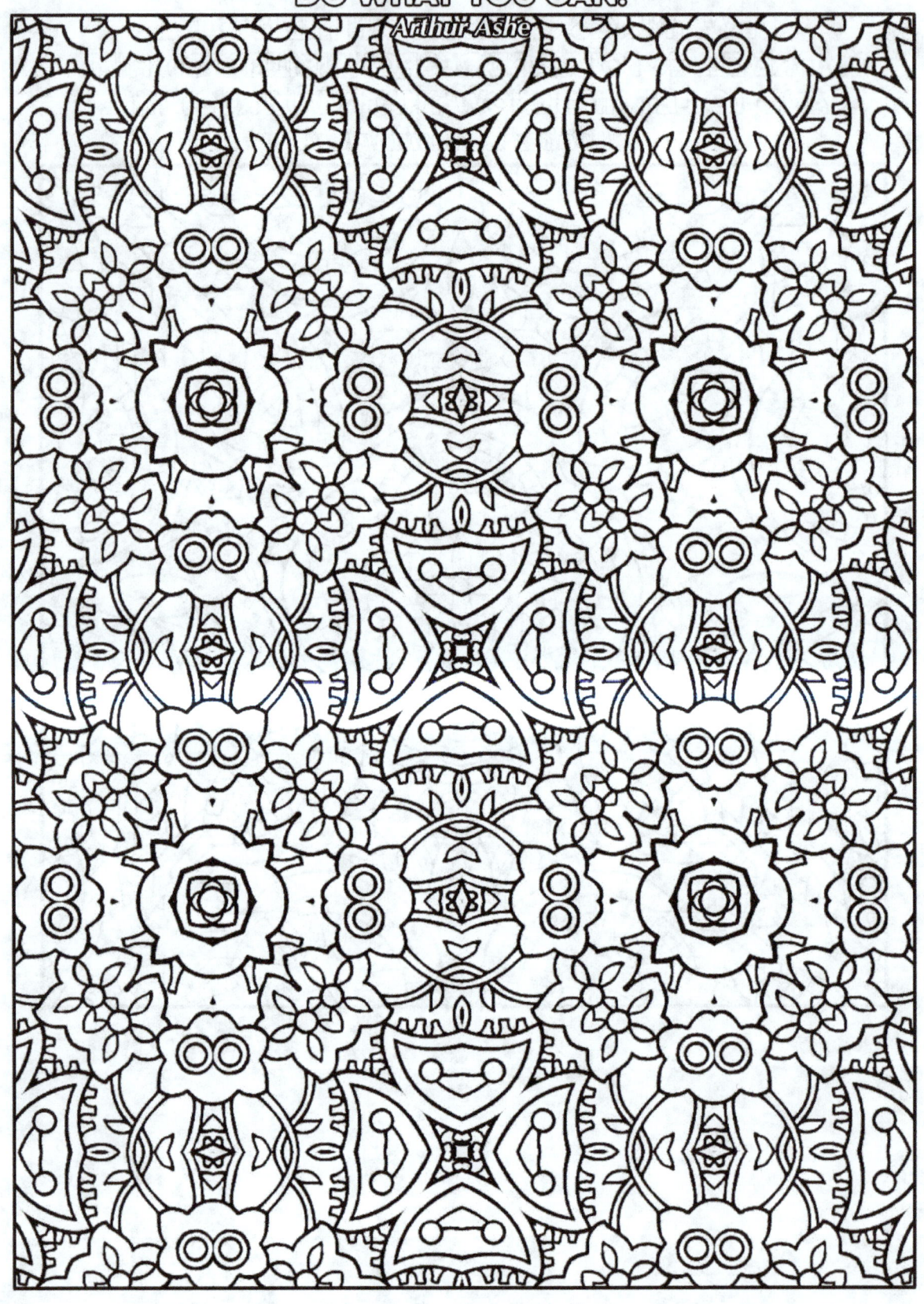

BELIEVE YOU CAN AND YOU'RE HALFWAY THERE.
Theodore Roosevelt

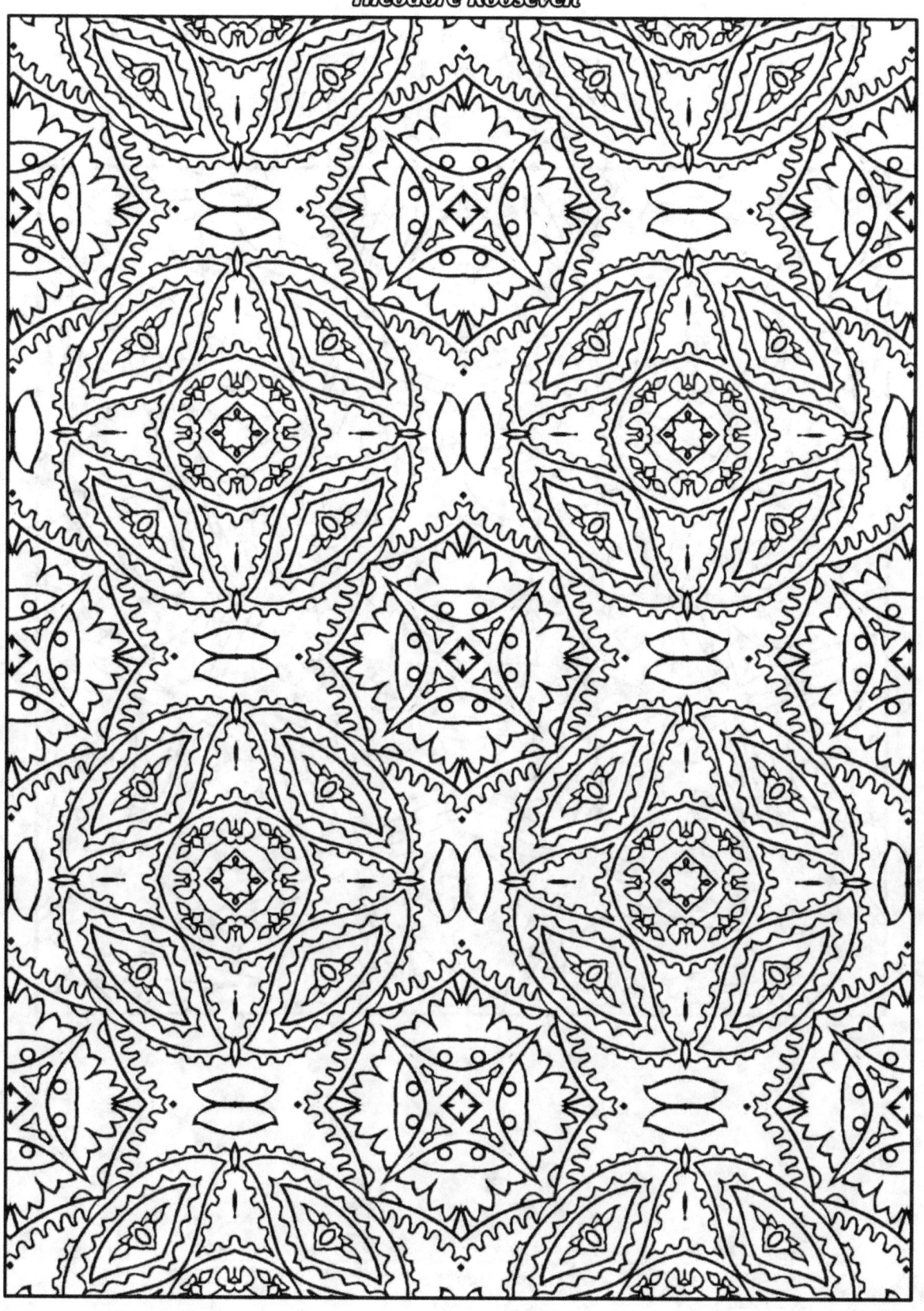

CHALLENGES ARE WHAT MAKE LIFE INTERESTING AND OVERCOMING THEM IS WHAT MAKES LIFE MEANINGFUL.

Joshua J. Marine

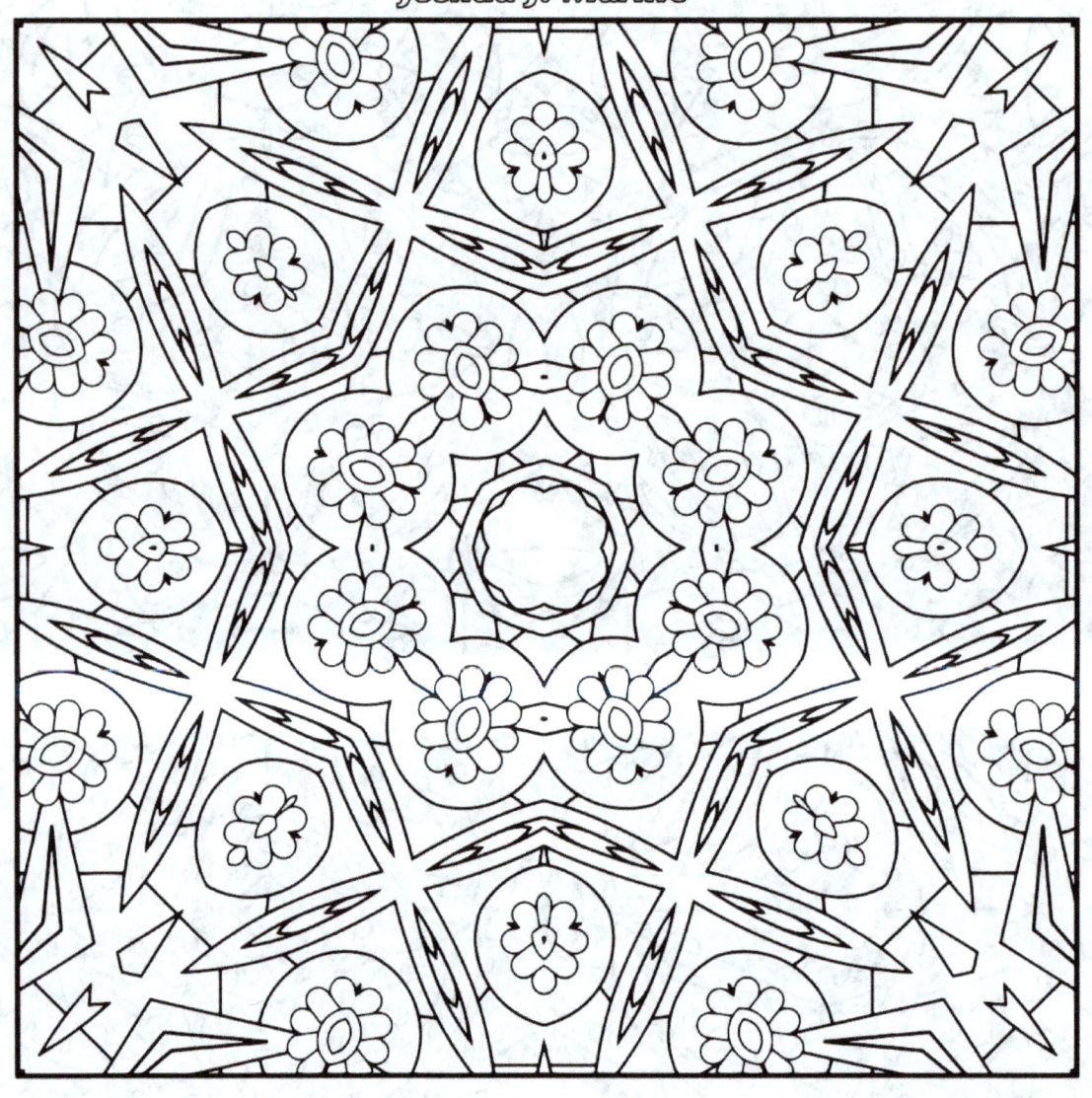

WE CAN EASILY FORGIVE A CHILD
WHO IS AFRAID OF THE DARK;
THE REAL TRAGEDY OF LIFE
IS WHEN MEN ARE AFRAID OF THE LIGHT.
Plato

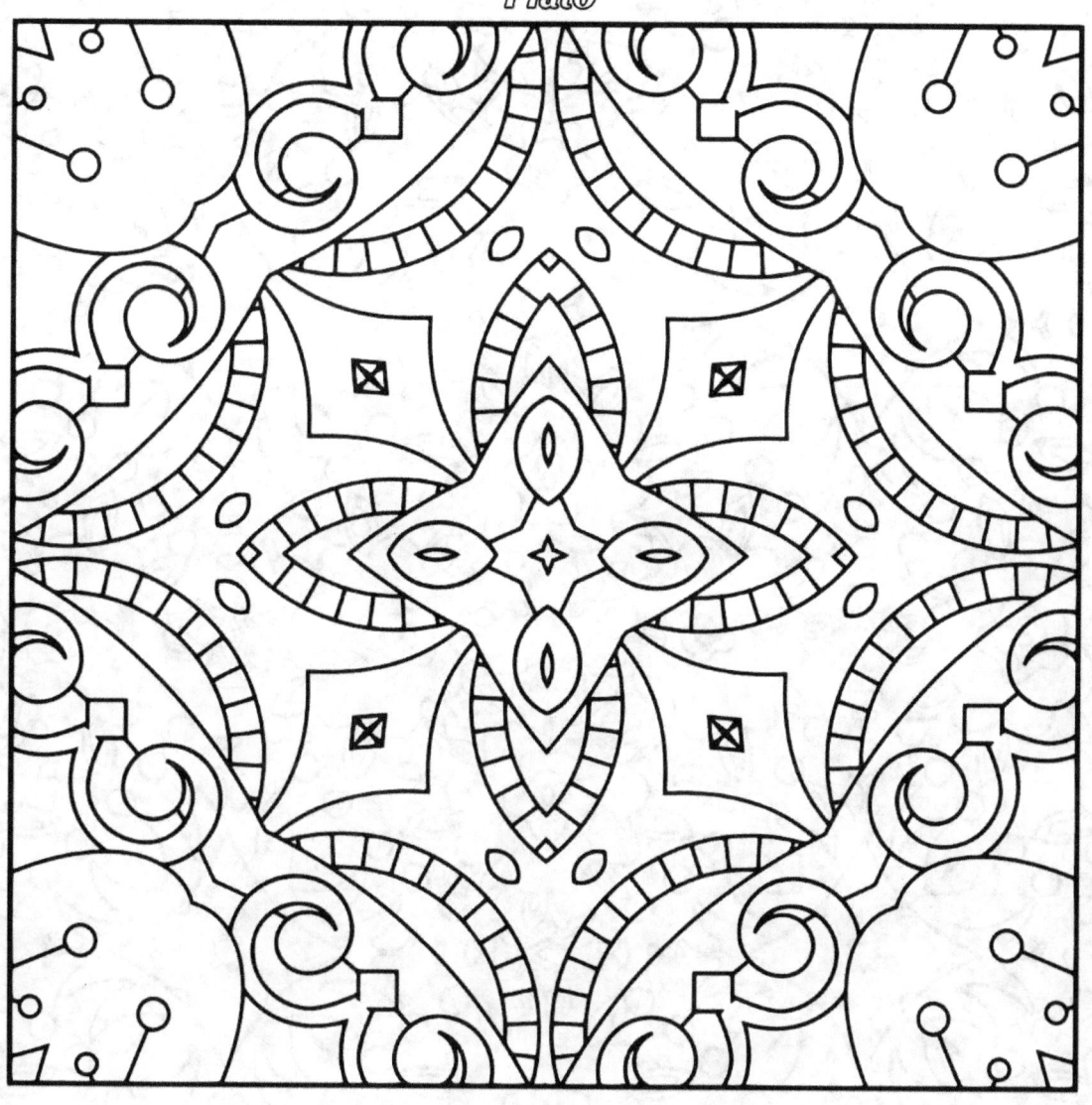

IT IS NEVER TOO LATE TO BE
WHAT YOU MIGHT HAVE BEEN.
George Eliot

EIGHTY PERCENT OF SUCCESS IS SHOWING UP.
Woody Allen

YOU CAN NEVER CROSS THE OCEAN
UNTIL YOU HAVE THE COURAGE
TO LOSE SIGHT OF THE SHORE.
Christopher Columbus

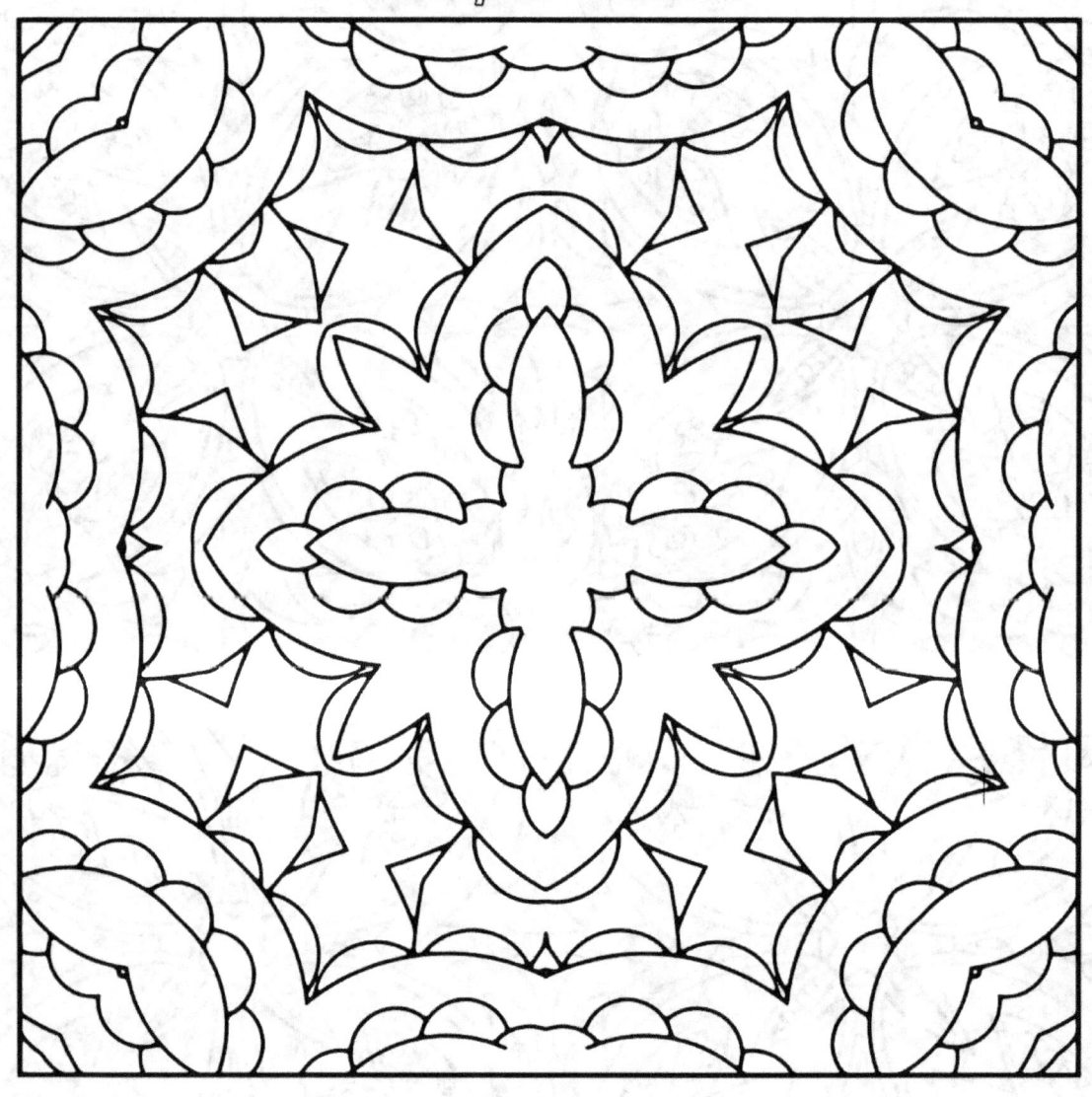

ASK AND IT WILL BE GIVEN TO YOU;
SEARCH, AND YOU WILL FIND;
KNOCK AND THE DOOR WILL BE OPENED FOR YOU.
Jesus Christ

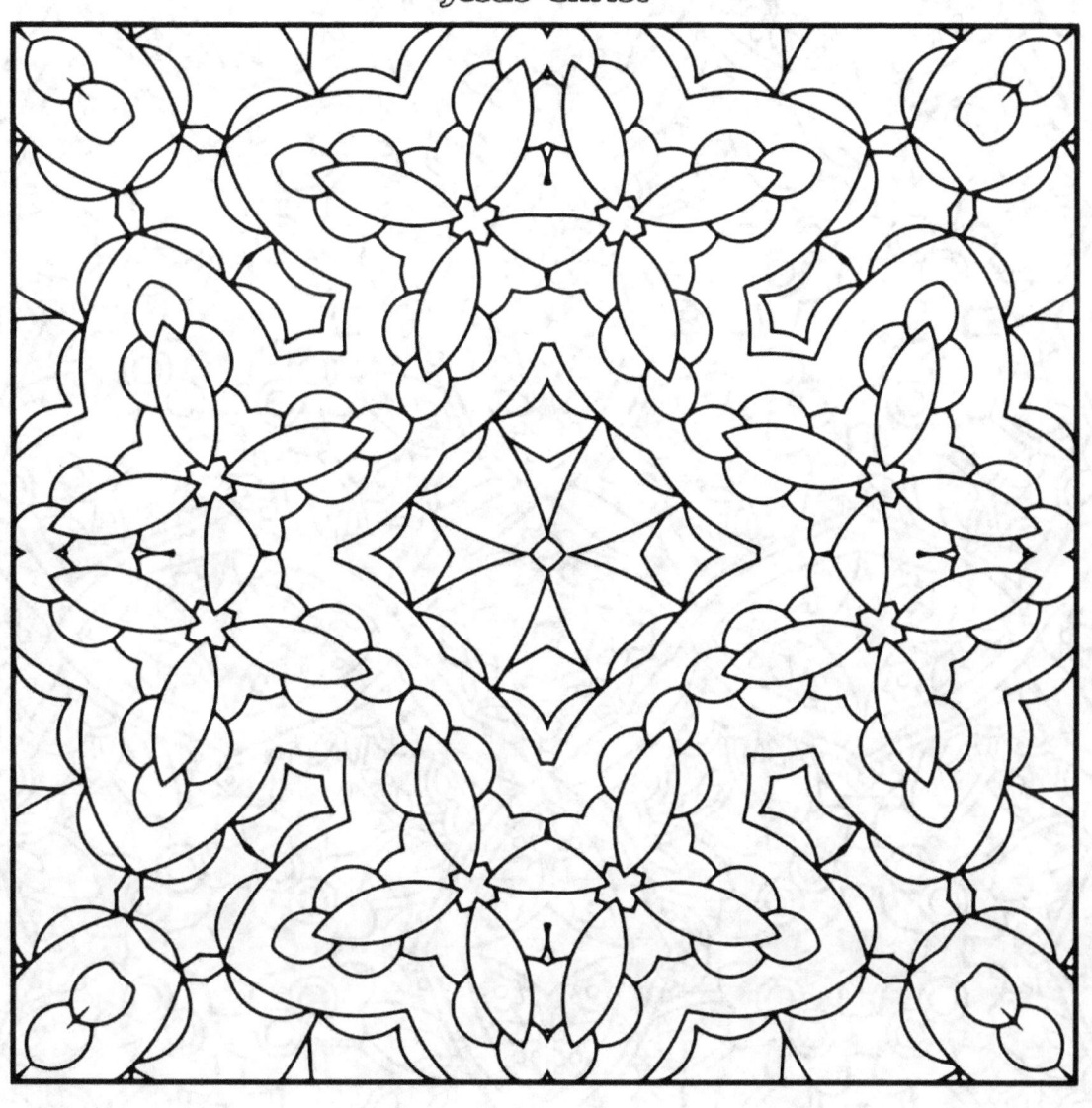

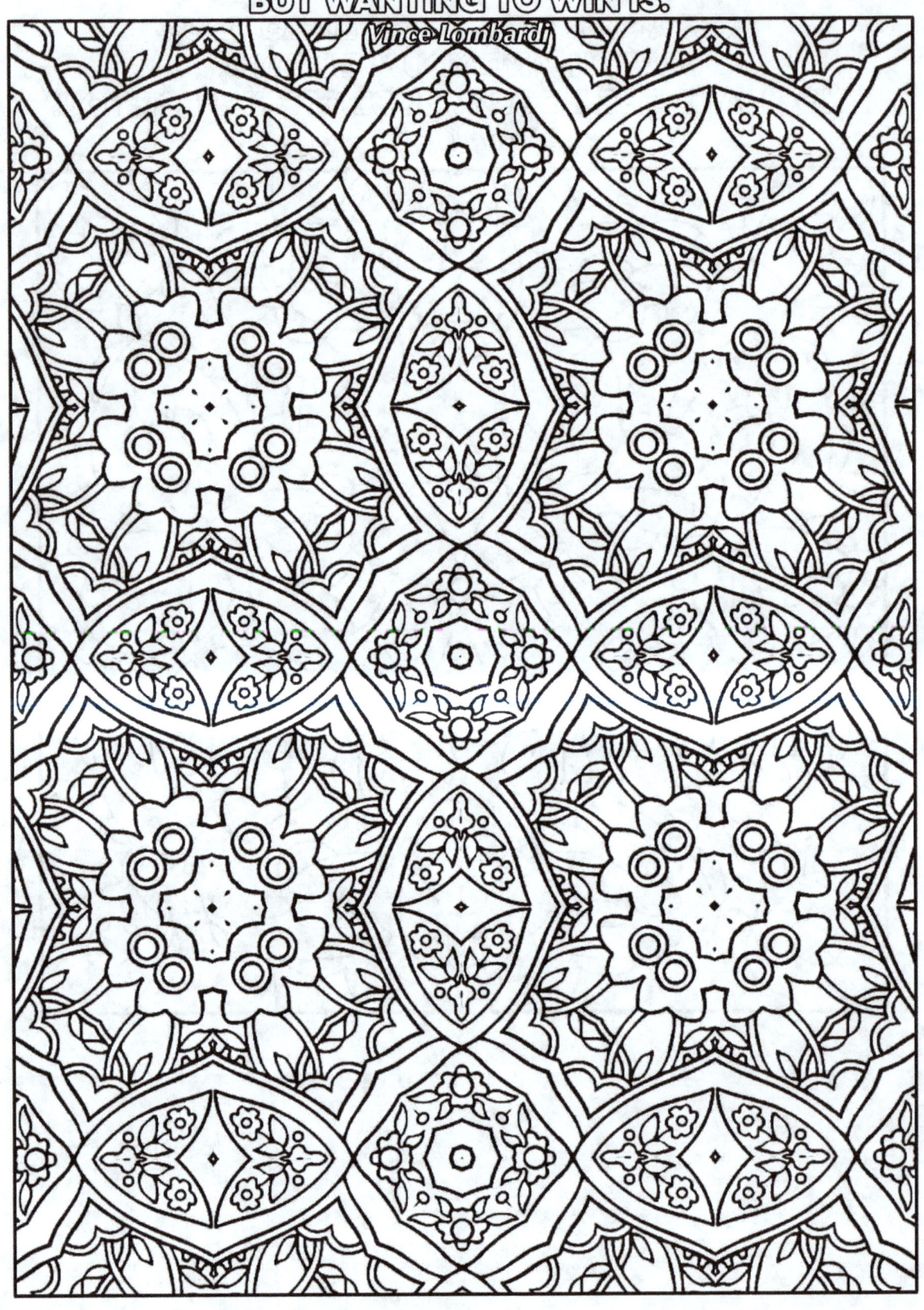

I AM NOT A PRODUCT OF MY CIRCUMSTANCES.
I AM A PRODUCT OF MY DECISIONS.

Stephen Covey

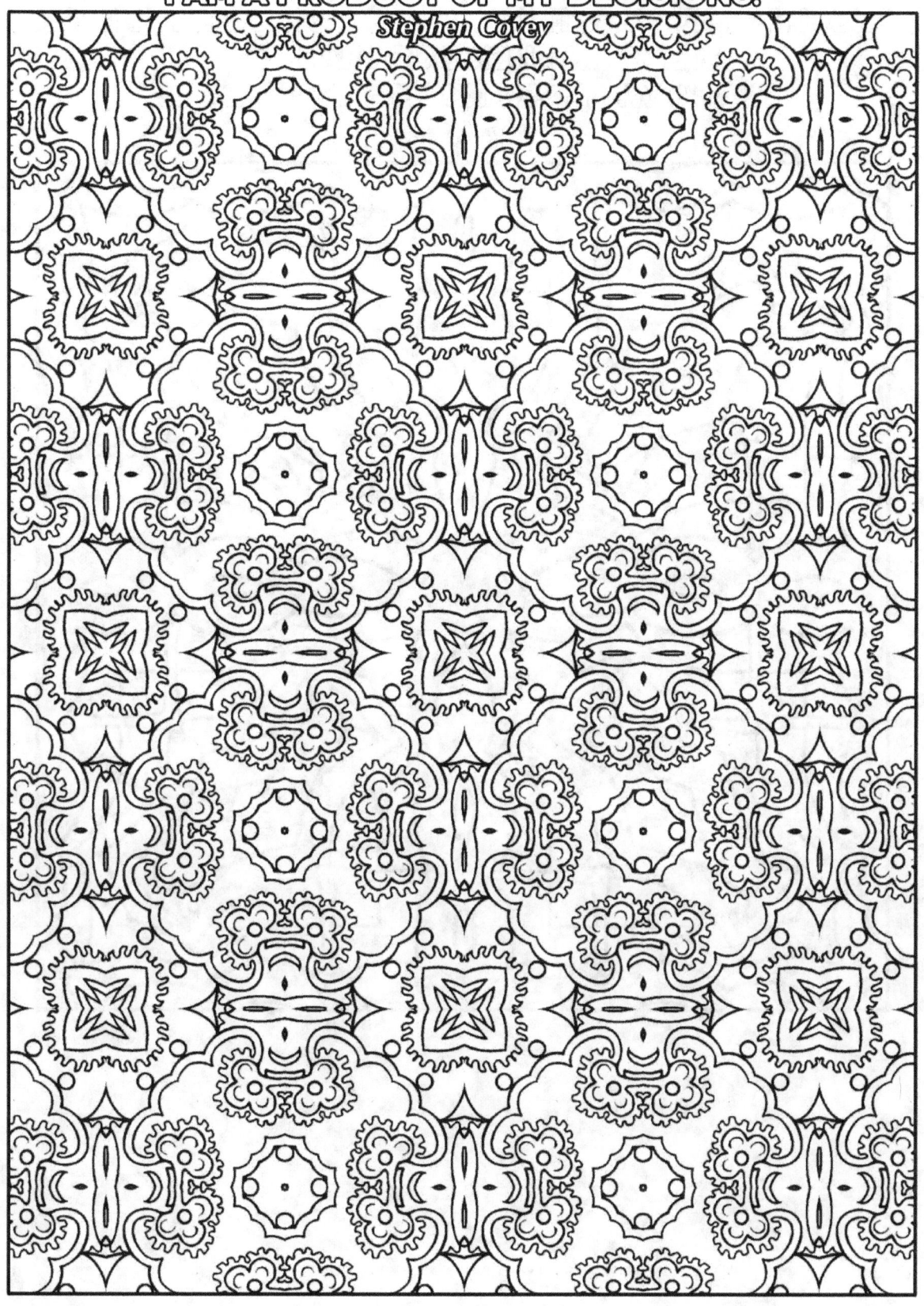

PEOPLE OFTEN SAY THAT MOTIVATION DOESN'T LAST.
WELL, NEITHER DOES BATHING.
THAT'S WHY WE RECOMMEND IT DAILY.
Zig Ziglar

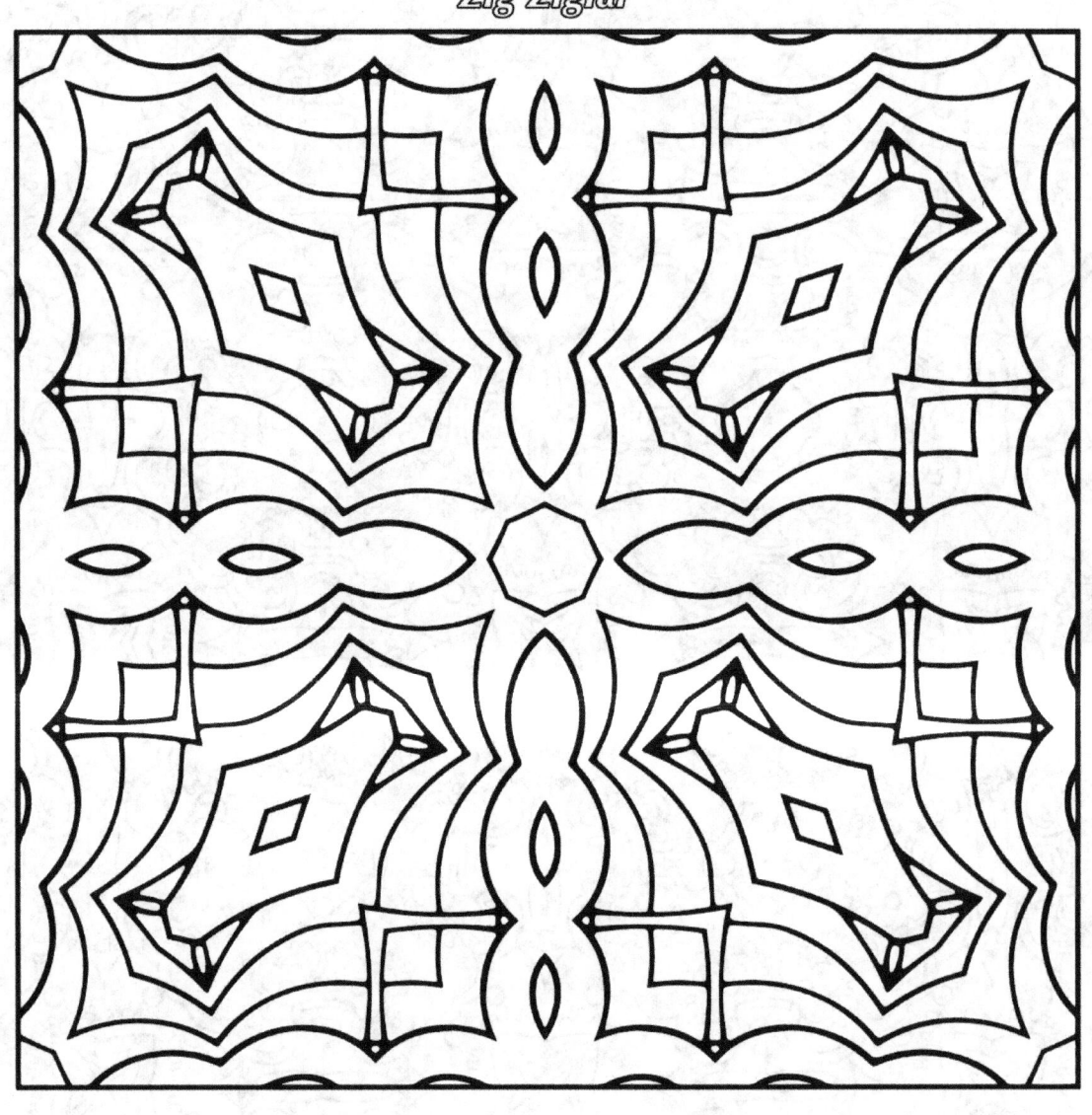

THE TWO MOST IMPORTANT DAYS IN YOUR LIFE
ARE THE DAY YOU ARE BORN
AND THE DAY YOU FIND OUT WHY.
Mark Twain

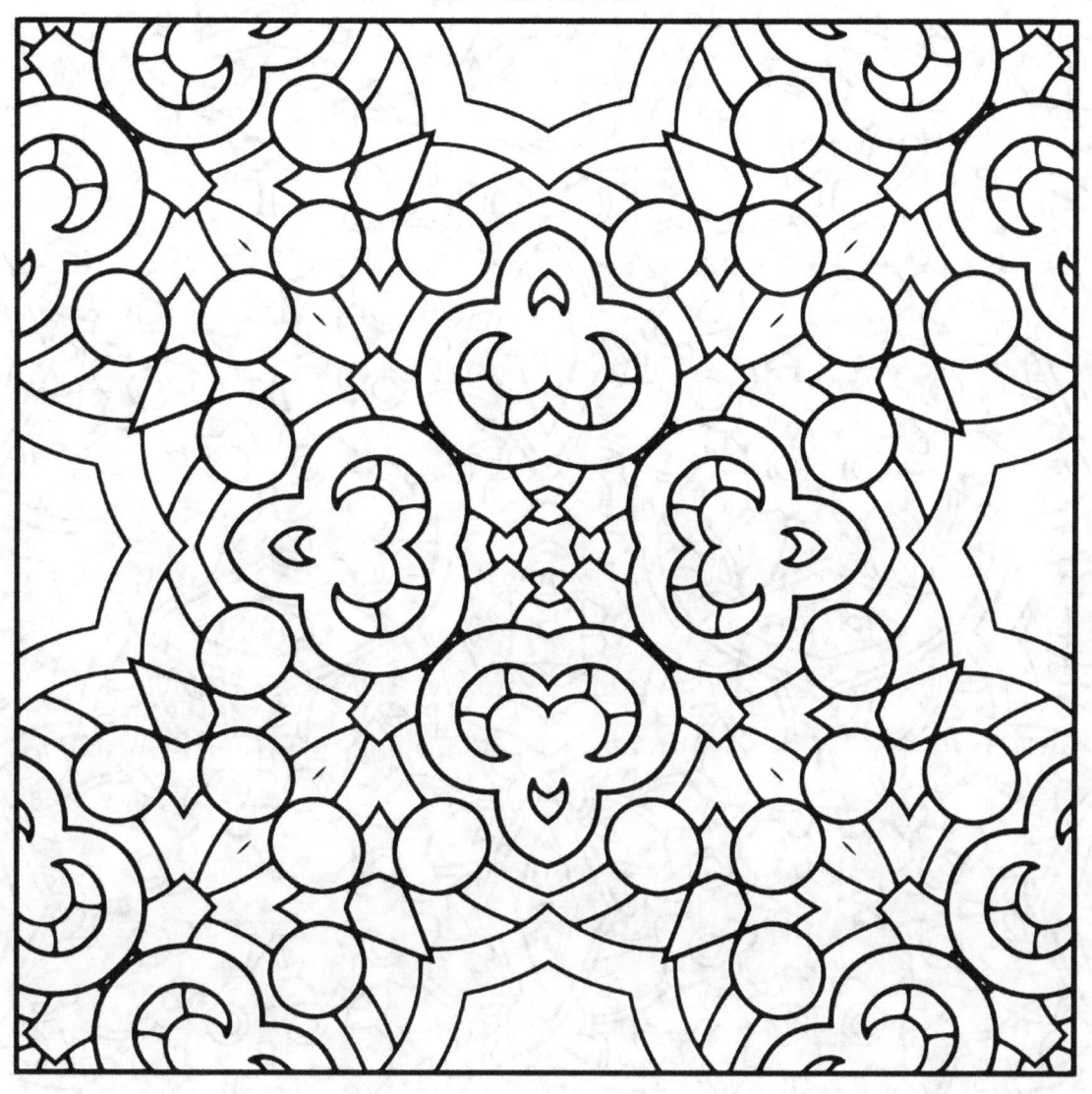

WE BECOME WHAT WE THINK ABOUT.
Earl Nightingale

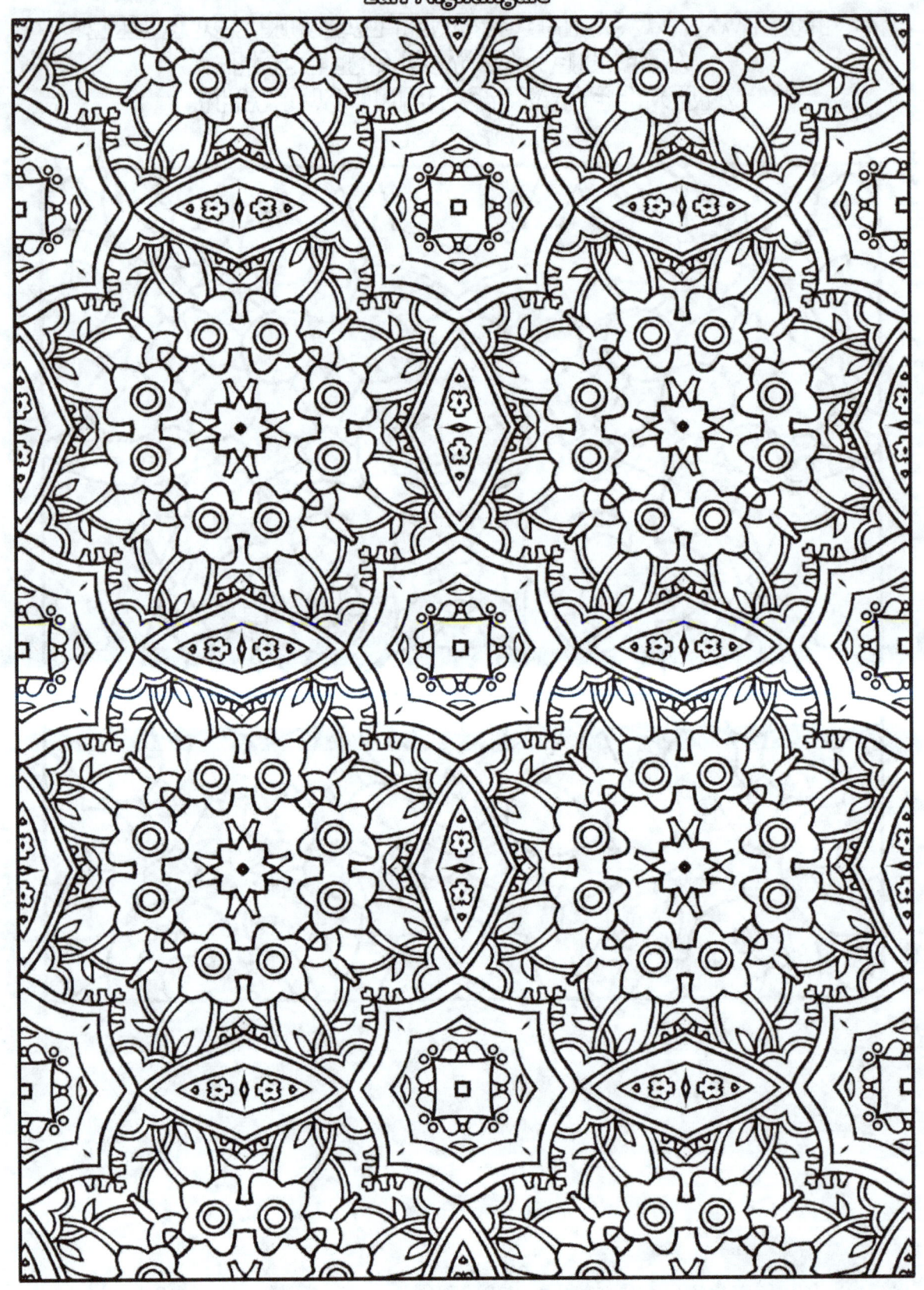

**LIFE IS 10% WHAT HAPPENS TO ME
AND 90% OF HOW I REACT TO IT.**
Charles Swindoll

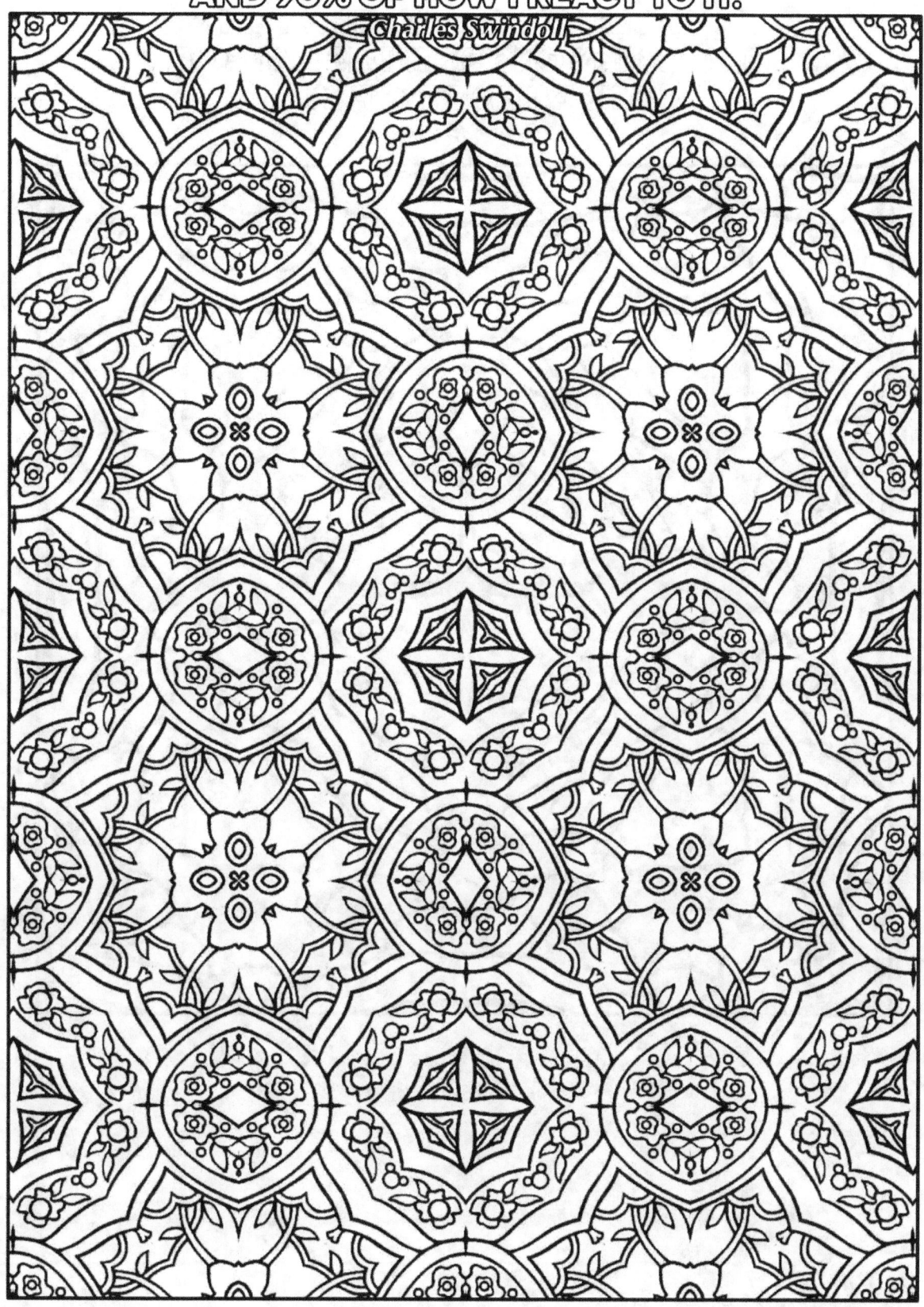

**I HAVE LEARNED OVER THE YEARS
THAT WHEN ONE'S MIND IS MADE UP,
THIS DIMINISHES FEAR.**
Rosa Parks

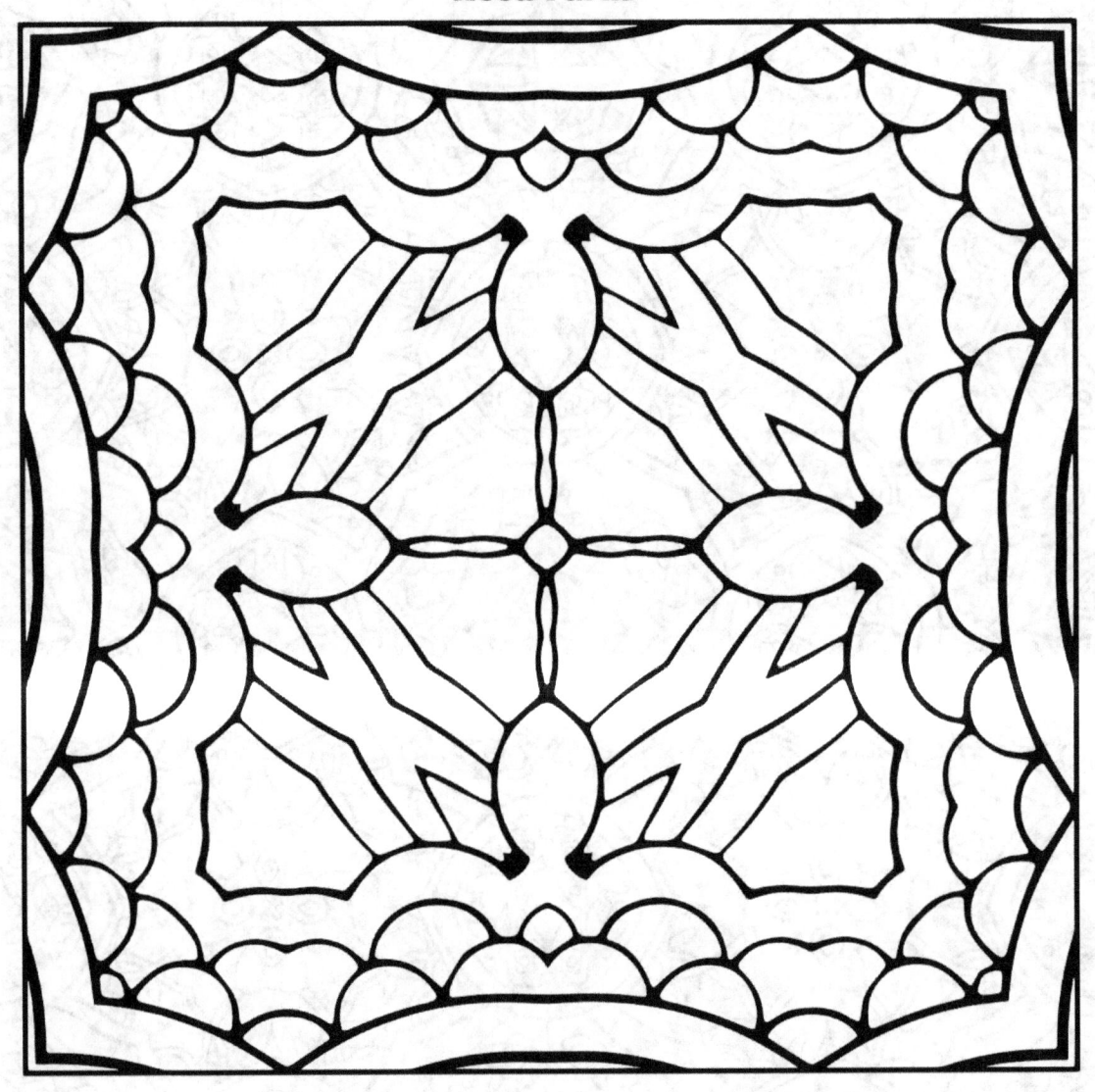

**THE PERSON WHO SAYS IT CANNOT BE DONE
SHOULD NOT INTERRUPT
THE PERSON WHO IS DOING IT.**
Chinese Proverb

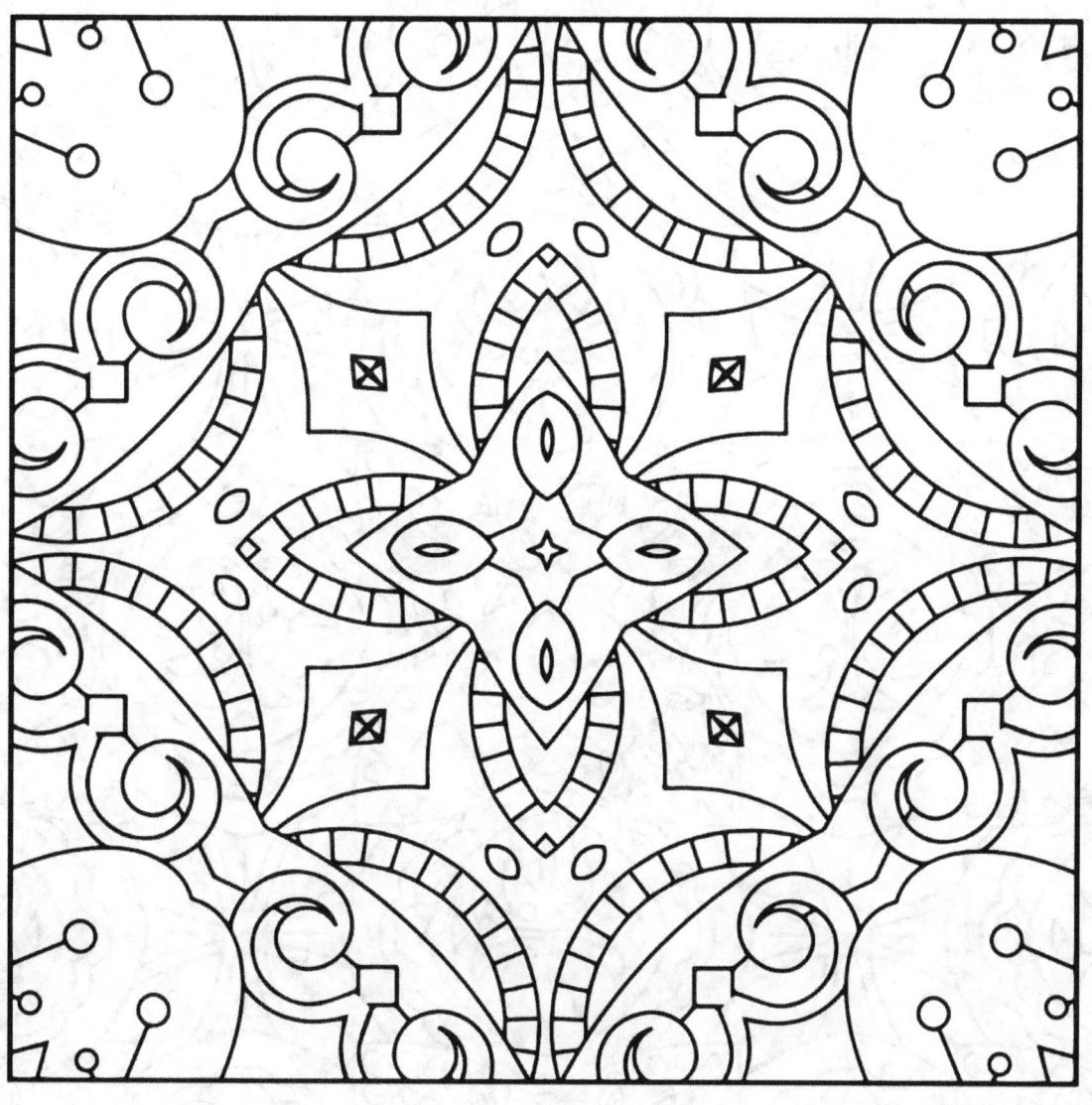

66

THE ONLY WAY TO DO GREAT WORK IS TO LOVE WHAT YOU DO.

Steve Jobs

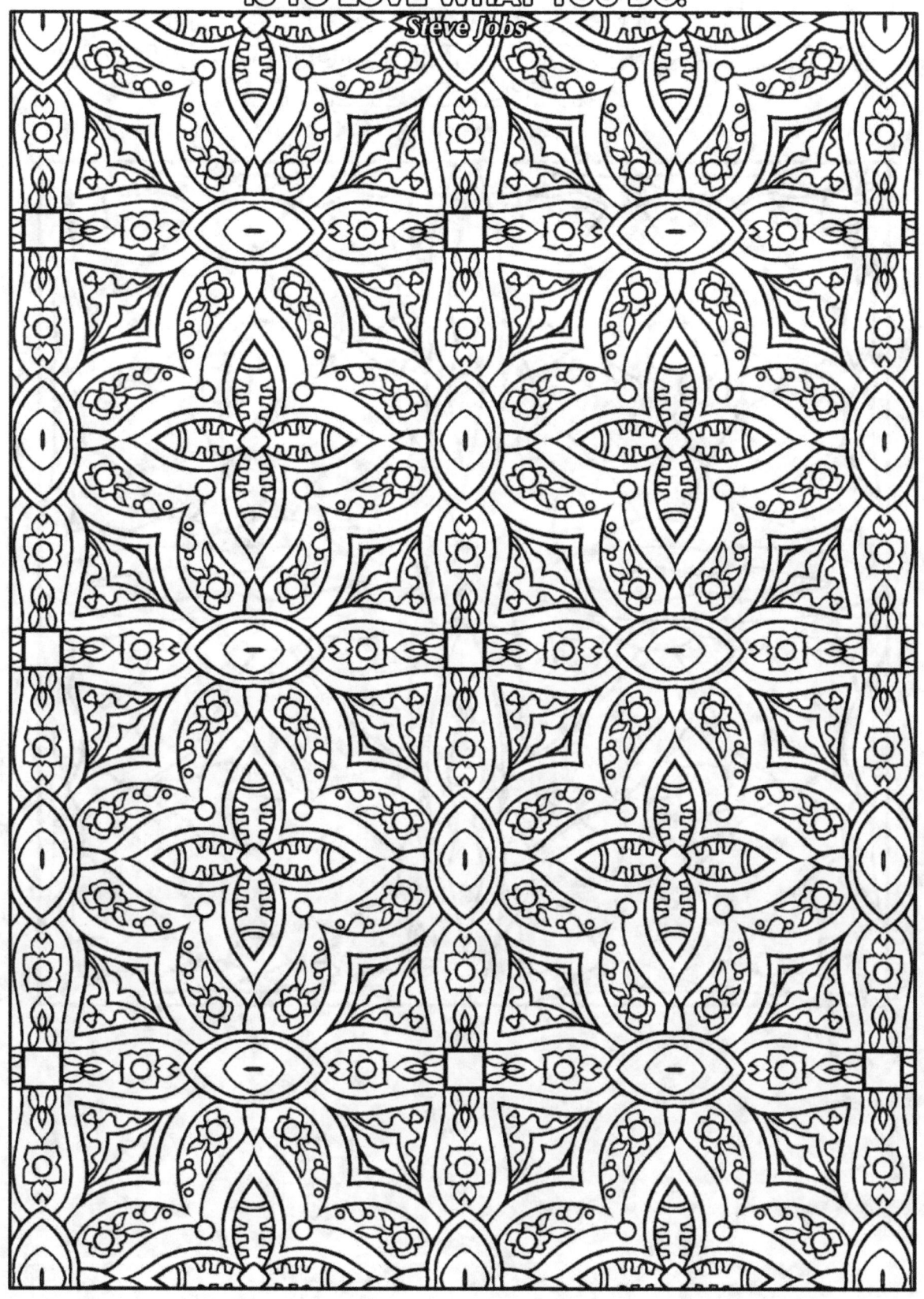

YOU CAN'T FALL IF YOU DON'T CLIMB.
BUT THERE'S NO JOY IN LIVING YOUR WHOLE LIFE
ON THE GROUND.
Unknown

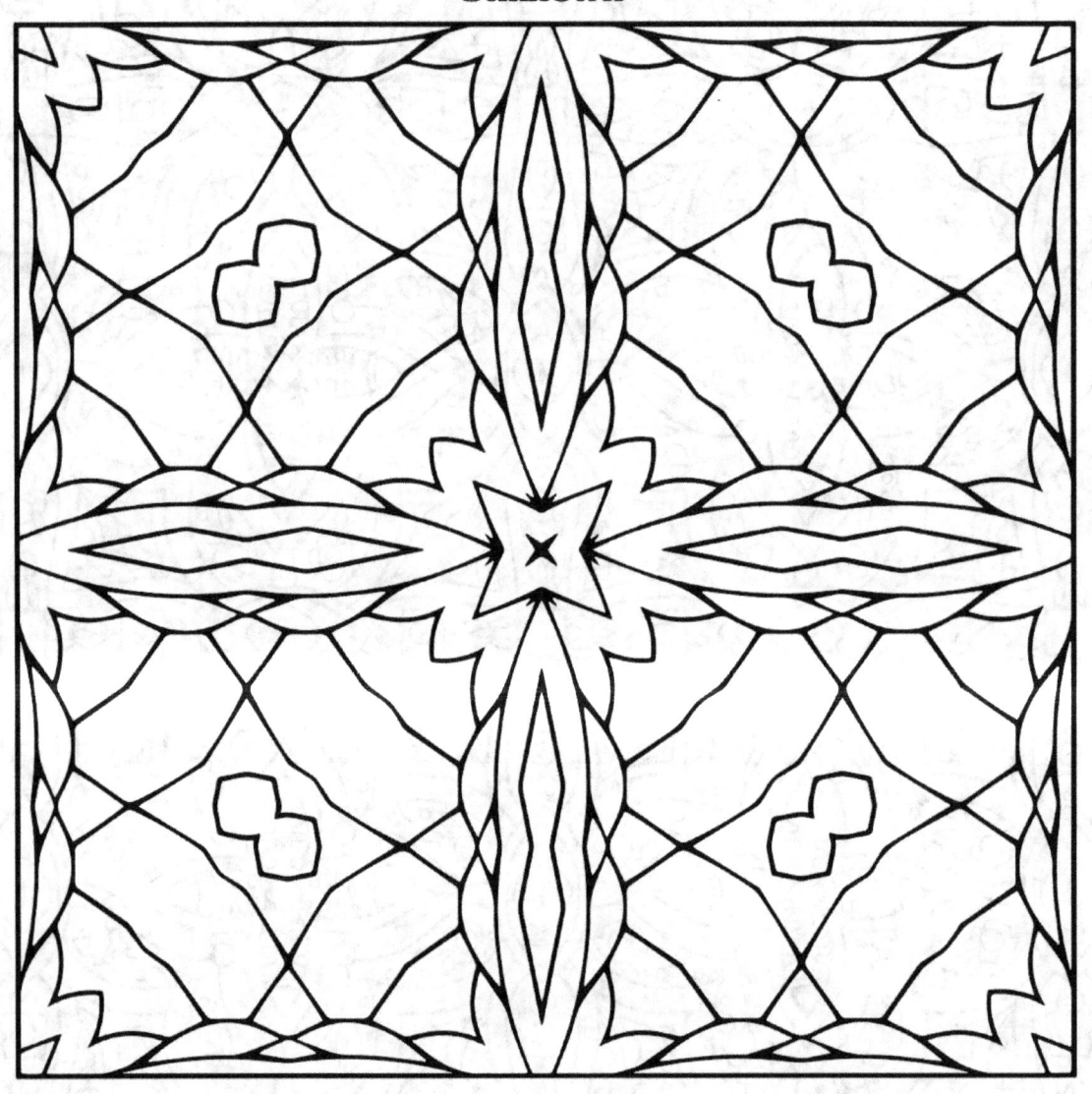

LIVE AS IF YOU WERE TO DIE TOMORROW.
LEARN AS IF YOU WERE TO LIVE FOREVER.
Mahatma Gandhi

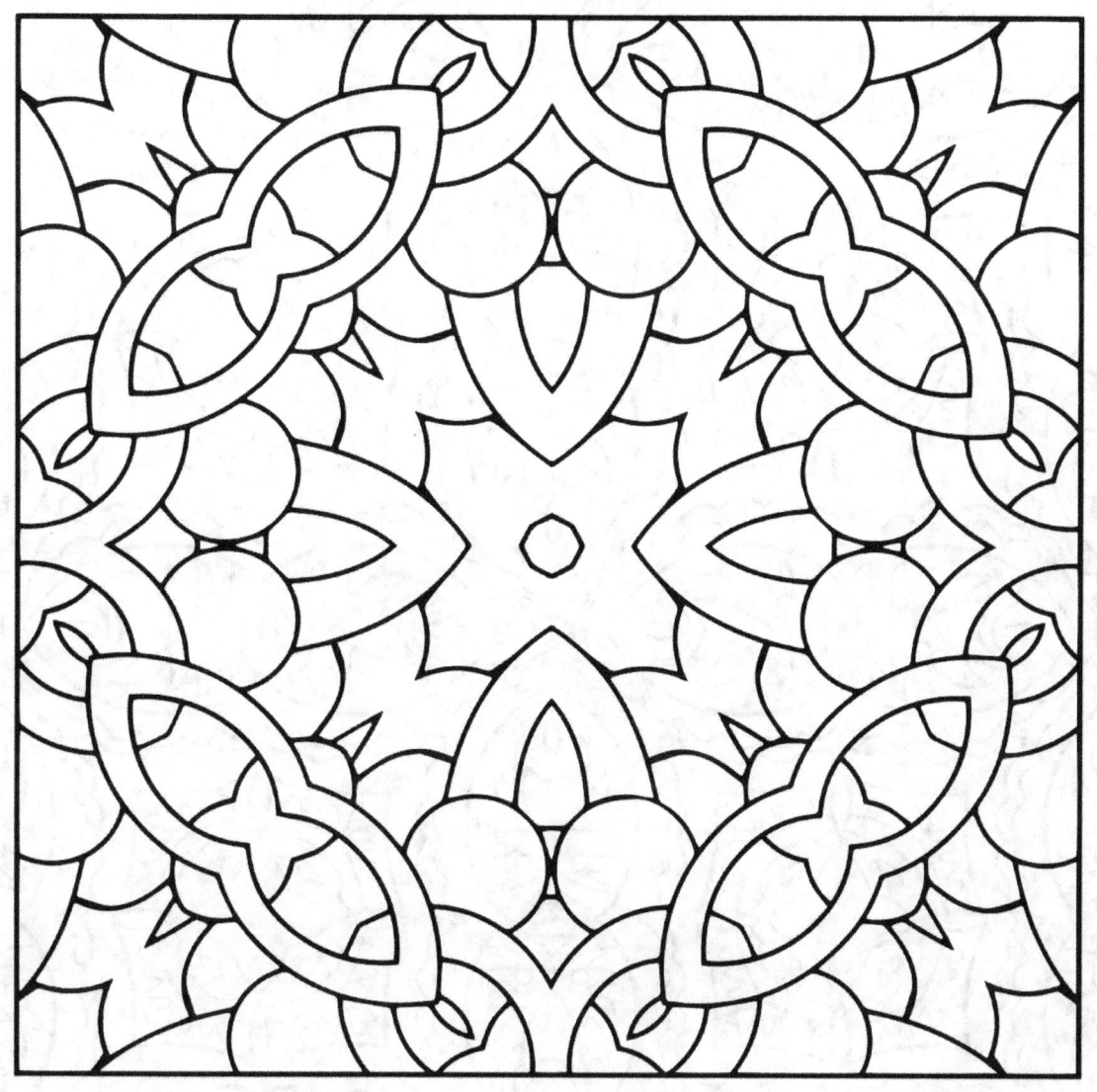

IF THE WIND WILL NOT SERVE, TAKE TO THE OARS.
Latin Proverb

EVERYTHING HAS BEAUTY,
BUT NOT EVERYONE CAN SEE.
Confucius

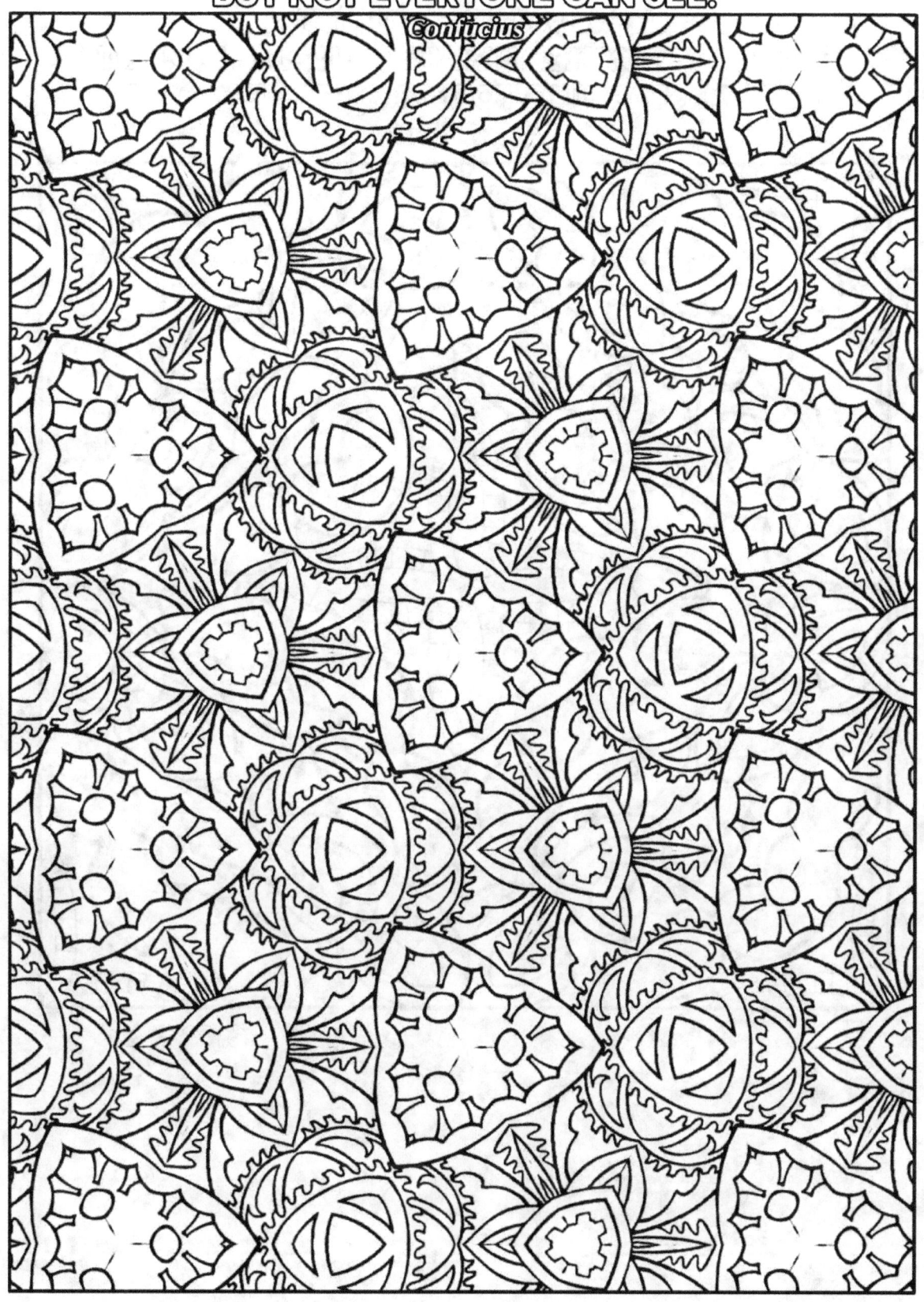

HOW WONDERFUL IT IS
THAT NOBODY NEED WAIT A SINGLE MOMENT
BEFORE STARTING TO IMPROVE THE WORLD.
Anne Frank

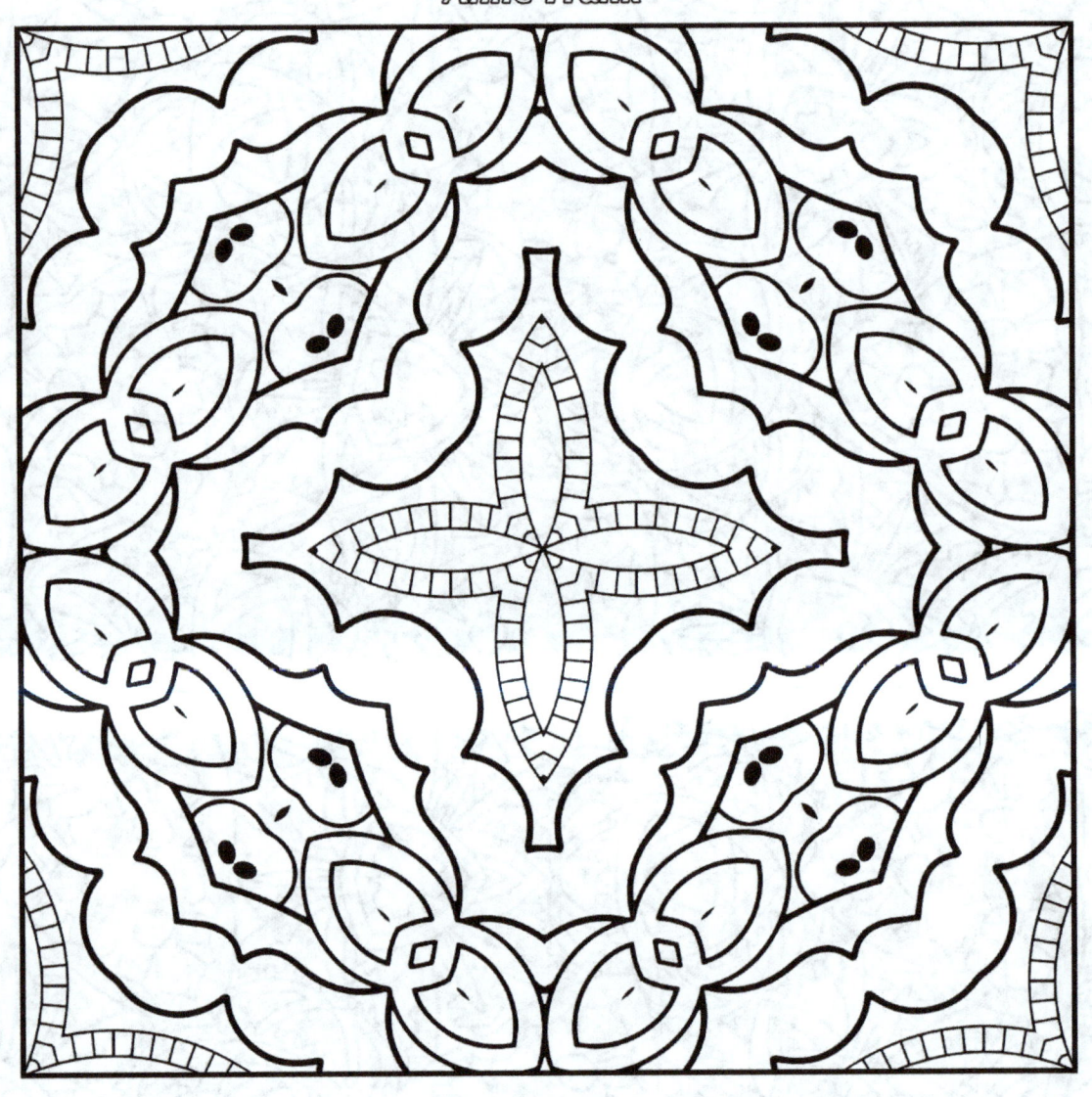

EVERY CHILD IS AN ARTIST.
THE PROBLEM IS HOW TO REMAIN AN ARTIST
ONCE HE GROWS UP.
Pablo Picasso

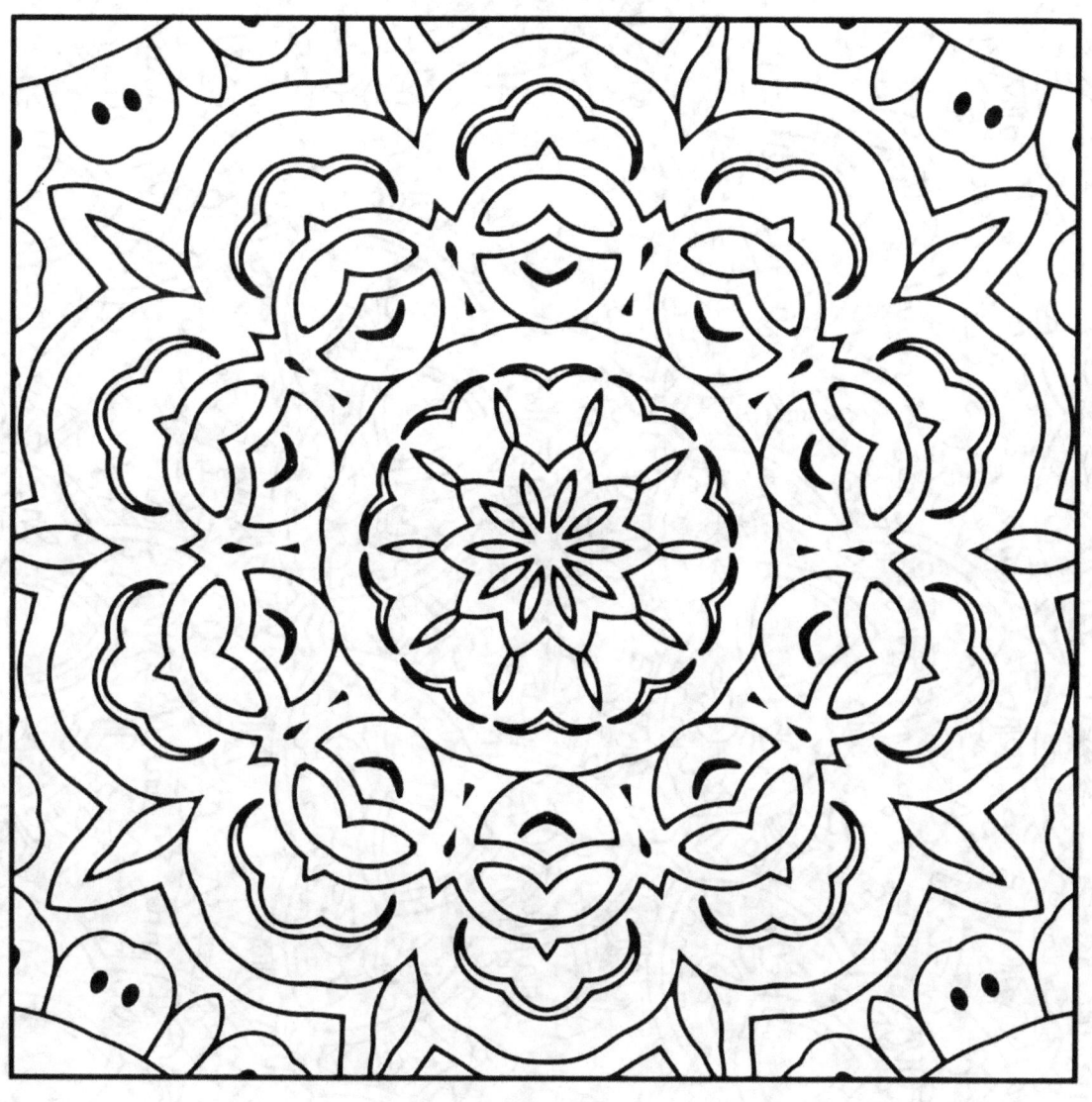

THE MIND IS EVERYTHING.
WHAT YOU THINK YOU BECOME.
Buddha

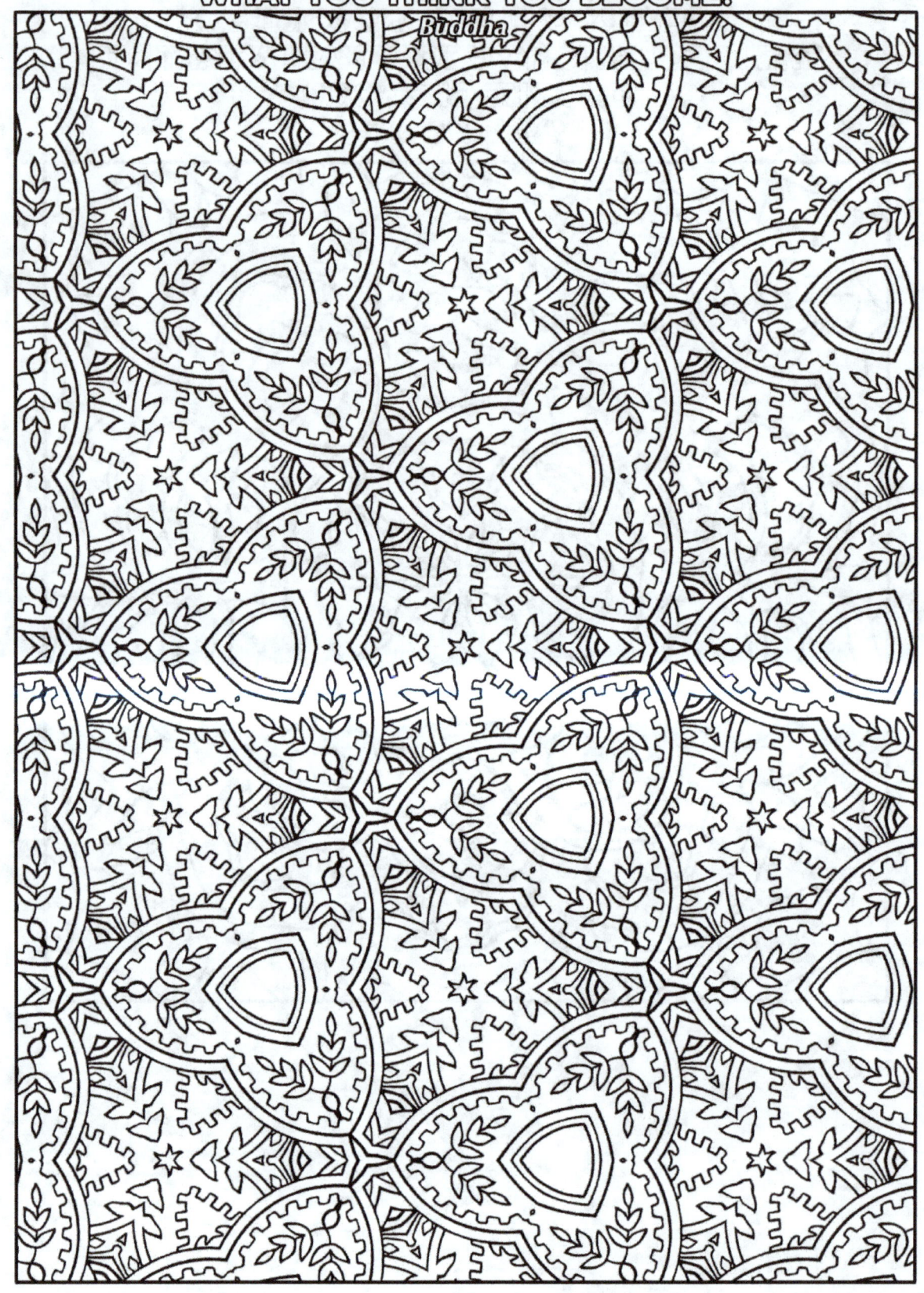

LIFE IS WHAT WE MAKE IT,
ALWAYS HAS BEEN, ALWAYS WILL BE.
Grandma Moses

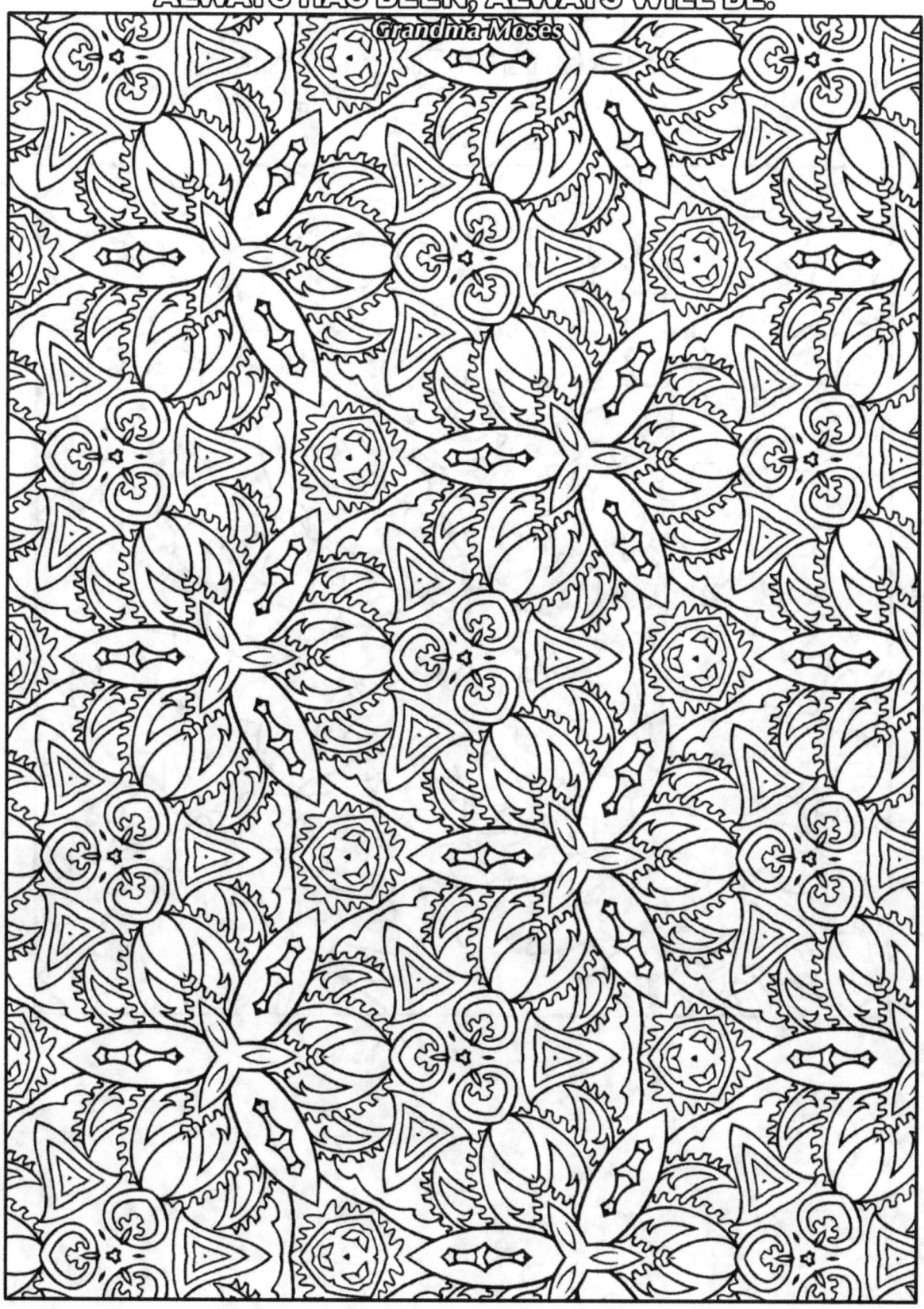

THE MOST COMMON WAY
PEOPLE GIVE UP THEIR POWER
IS BY THINKING THEY DON'T HAVE ANY.
Alice Walker

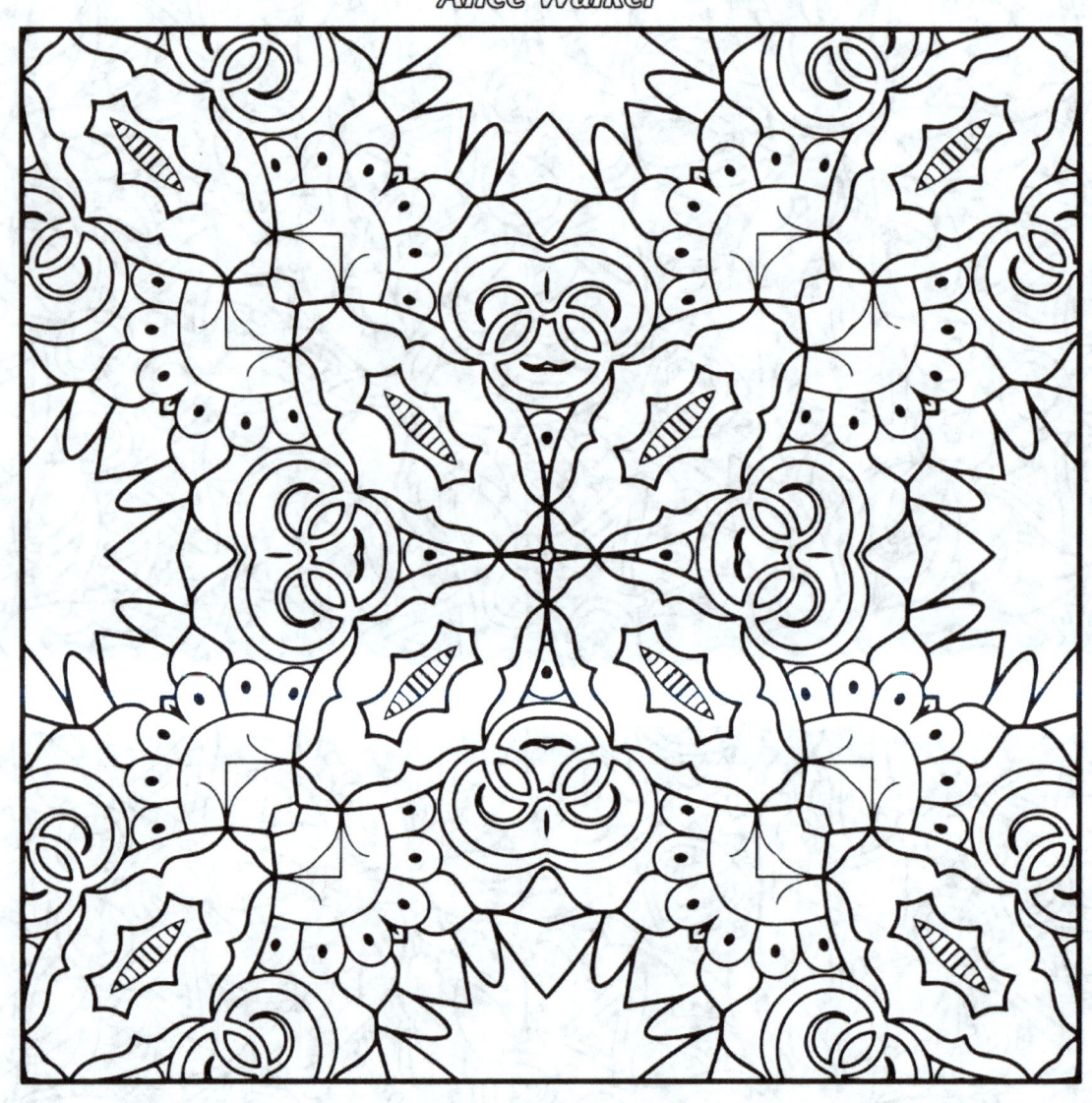

GO CONFIDENTLY
IN THE DIRECTION OF YOUR DREAMS.
LIVE THE LIFE YOU HAVE IMAGINED.
Henry David Thoreau

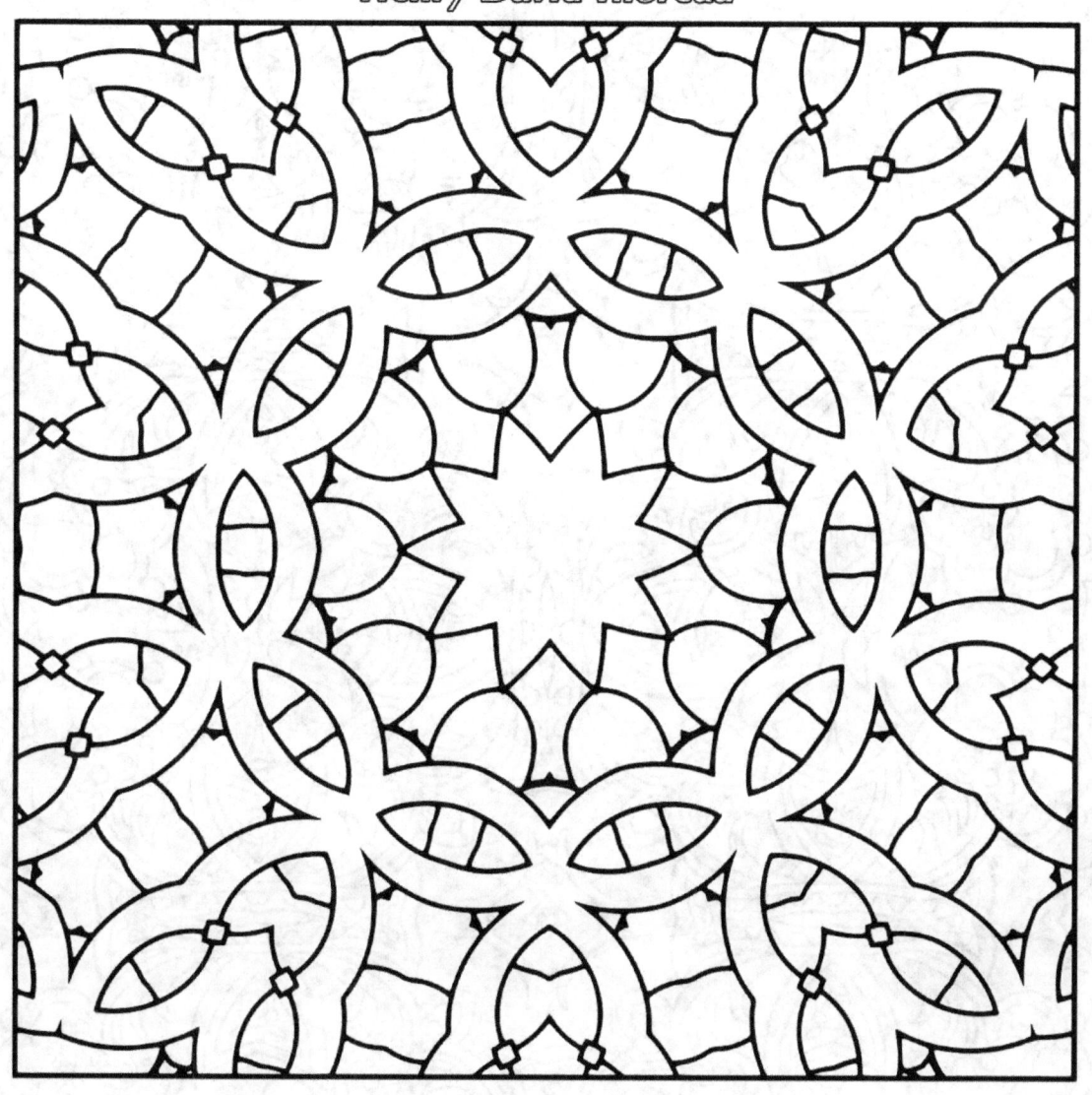

EVERY STRIKE BRINGS ME CLOSER
TO THE NEXT HOME RUN.
Babe Ruth

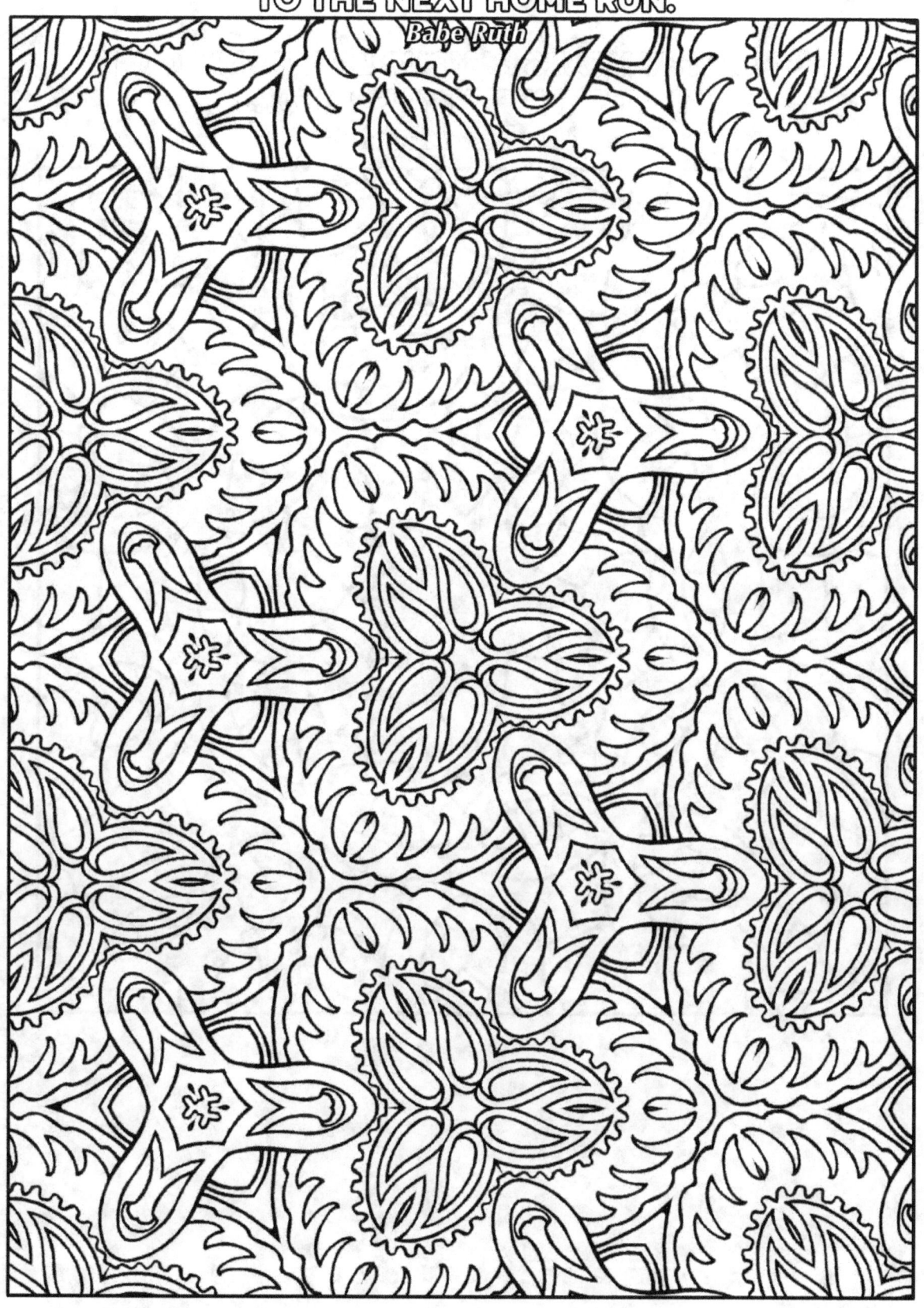

**IT'S NOT THE YEARS IN YOUR LIFE THAT COUNT.
IT'S THE LIFE IN YOUR YEARS.**
Abraham Lincoln

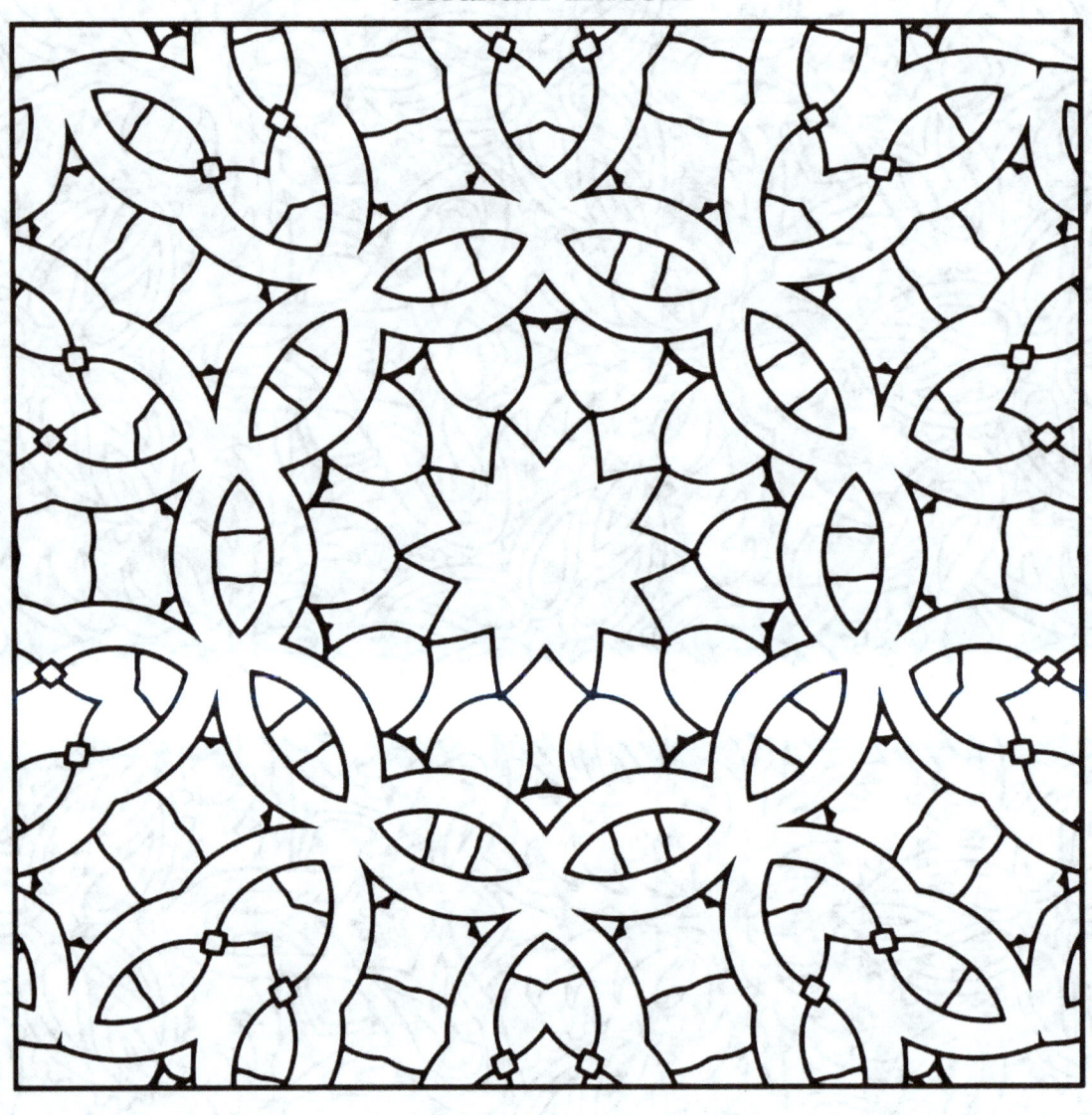

INSANITY:
DOING THE SAME THING OVER AND OVER AGAIN
AND EXPECTING DIFFERENT RESULTS.
Albert Einstein

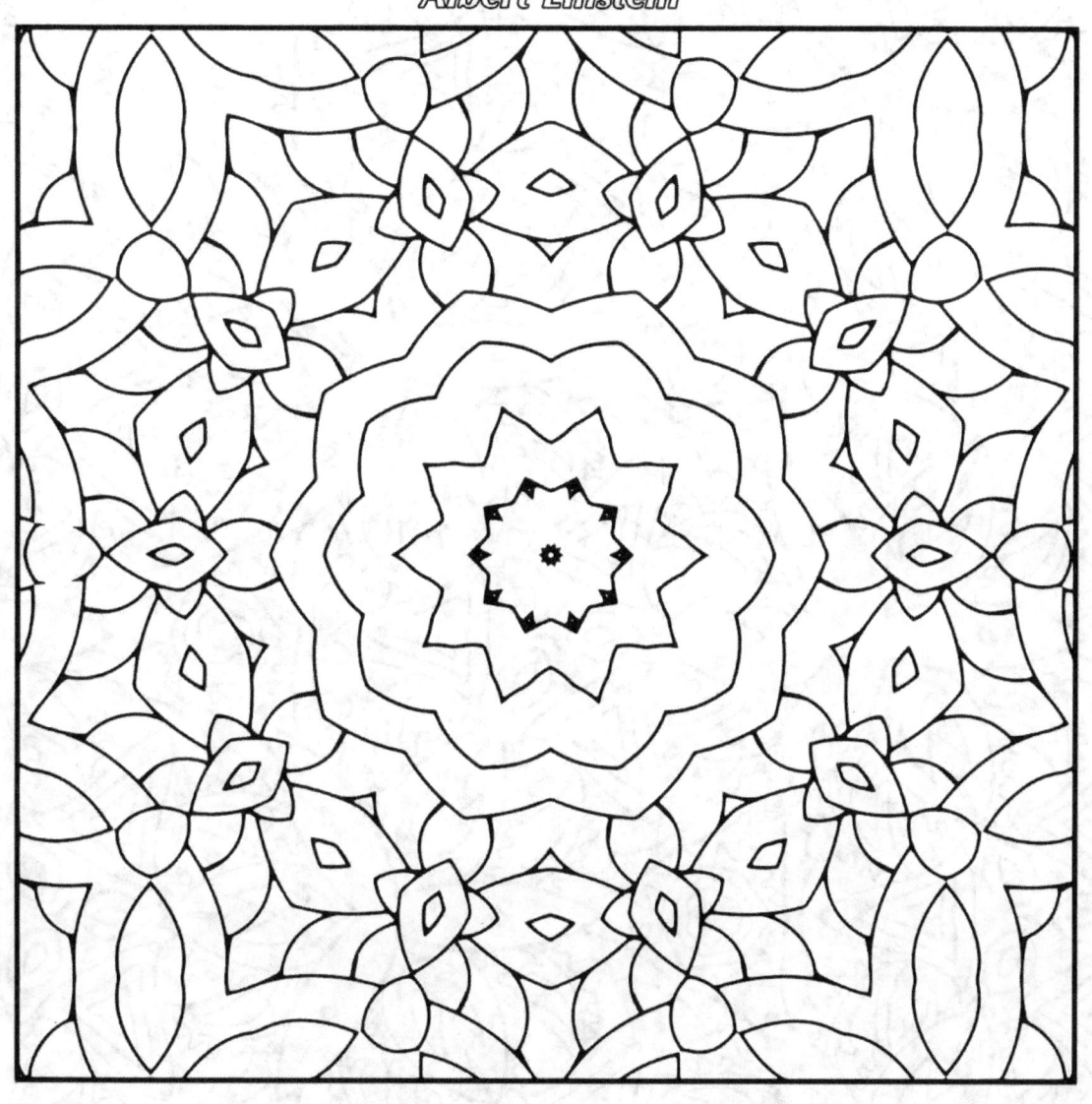

EITHER WRITE SOMETHING WORTH READING
OR DO SOMETHING WORTH WRITING.
Benjamin Franklin

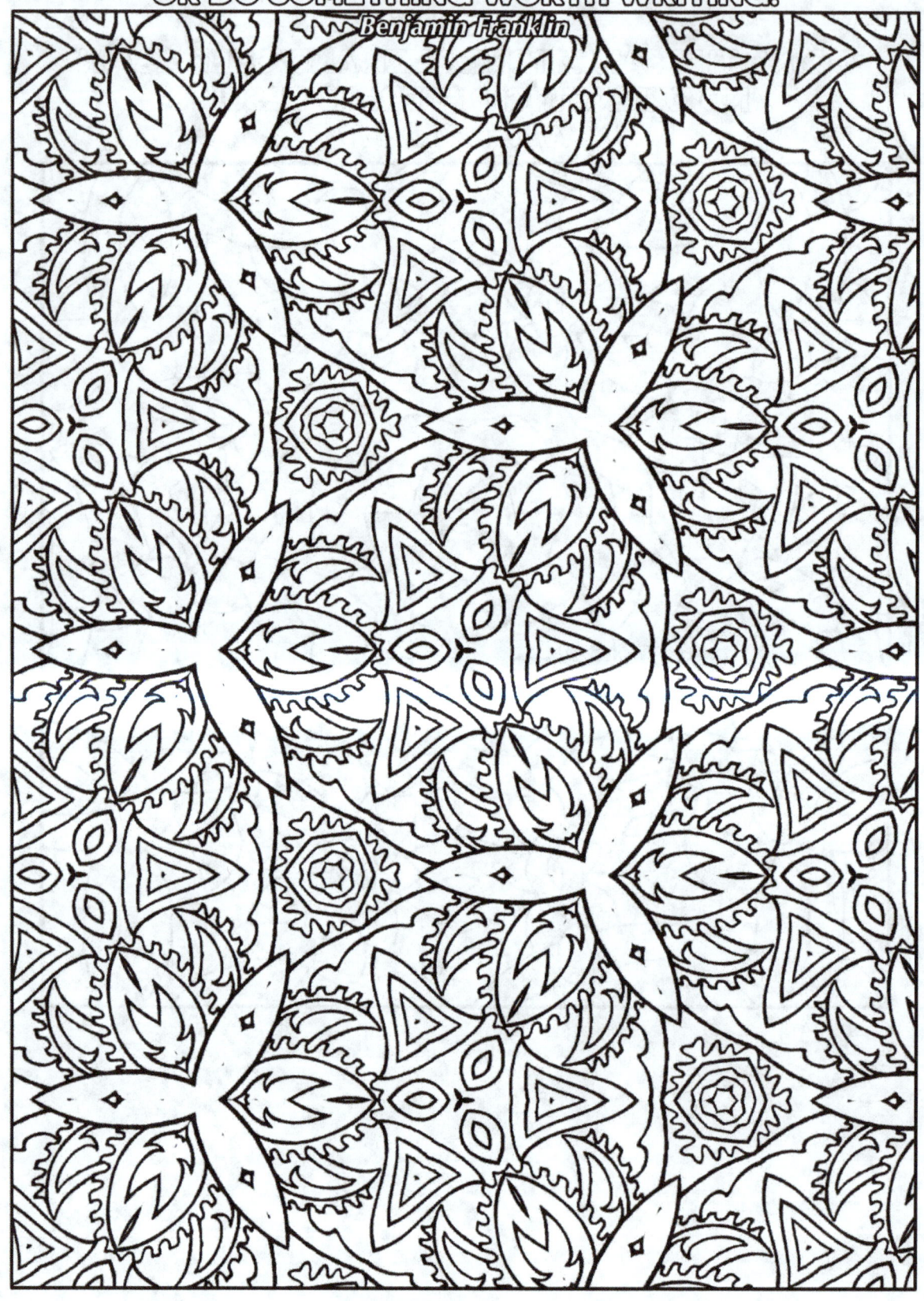

CHANGE YOUR THOUGHTS
AND YOU CHANGE YOUR WORLD.
Norman Vincent Peale

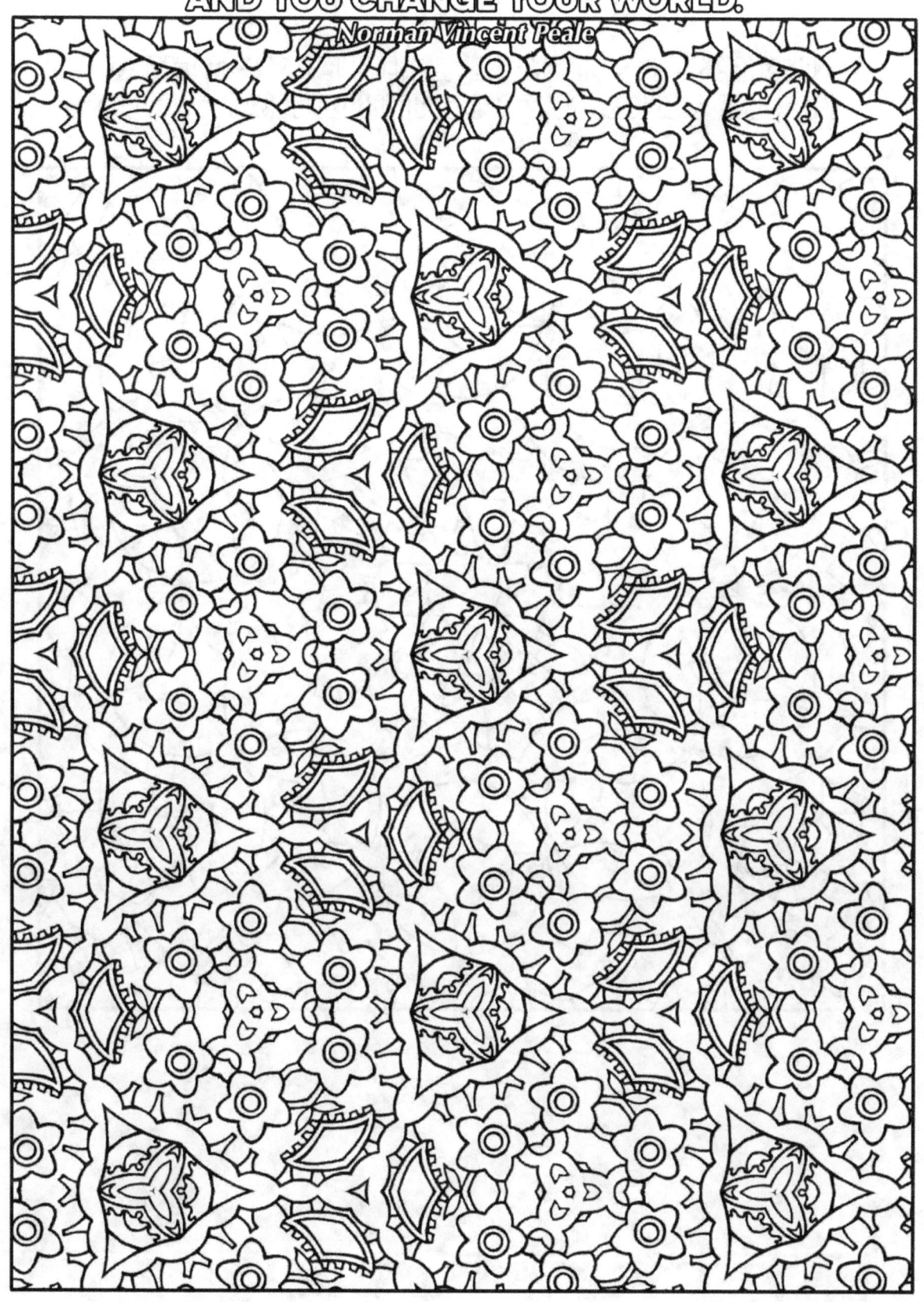

SUCCESS IS NOT FINAL, FAILURE IS NOT FATAL:
IT IS THE COURAGE TO CONTINUE THAT COUNTS.
Winston Churchill

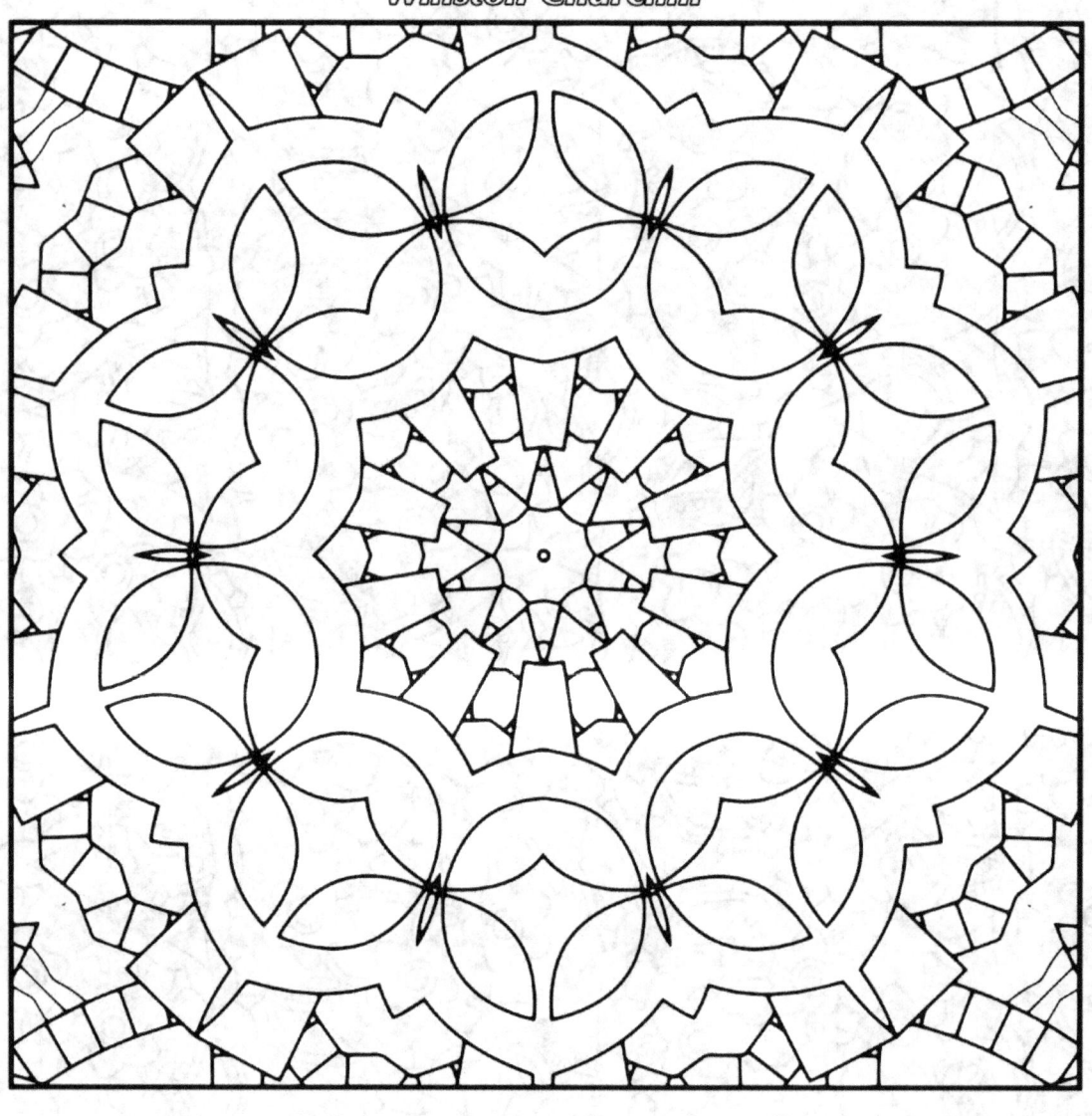

YOU HAVE ENEMIES?
GOOD.
THAT MEANS YOU'VE STOOD UP FOR SOMETHING,
SOMETIME IN YOUR LIFE.
Winston Churchill

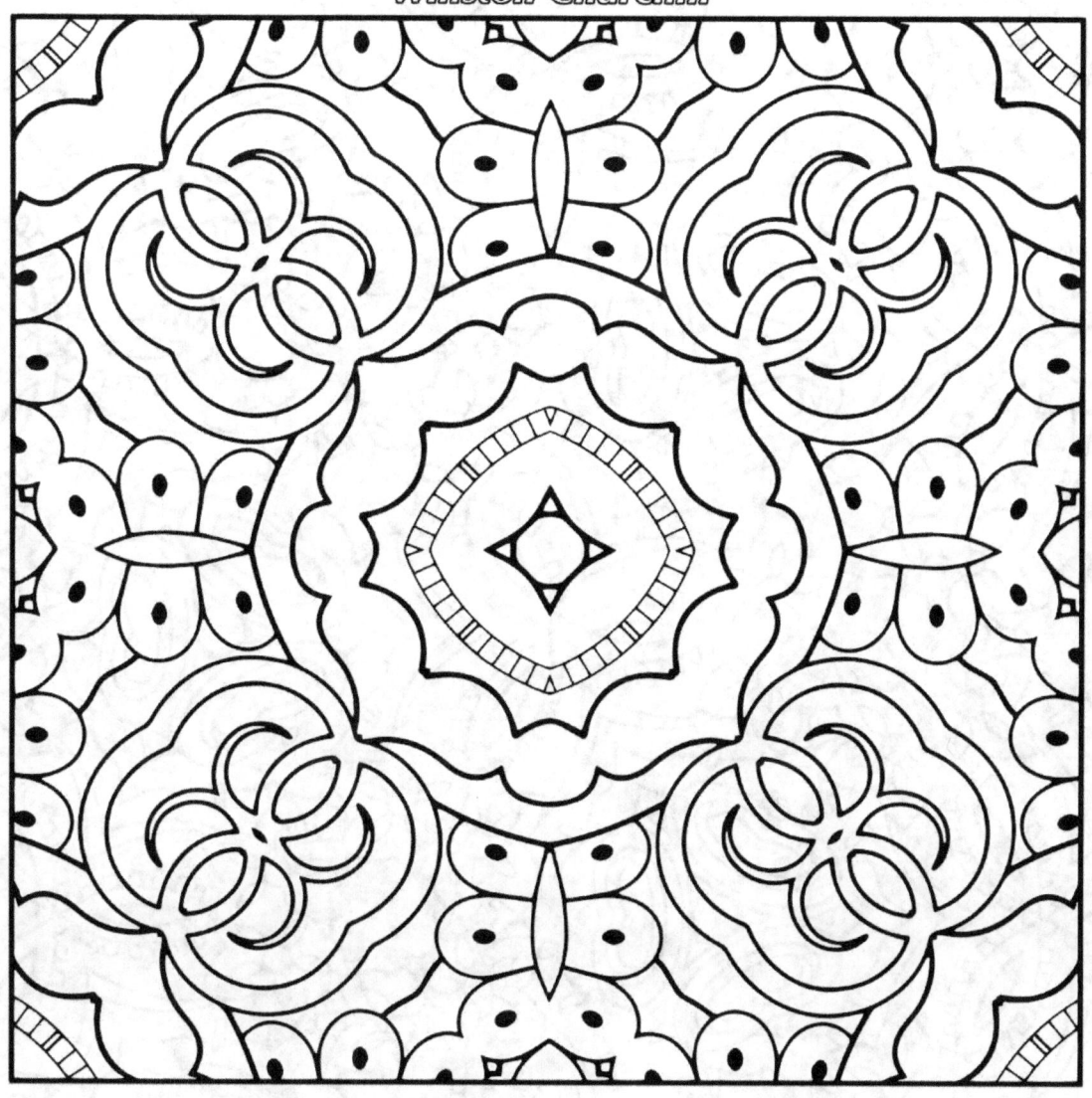

WHETHER YOU THINK YOU CAN
OR YOU THINK YOU CAN'T, YOU'RE RIGHT.
Henry Ford

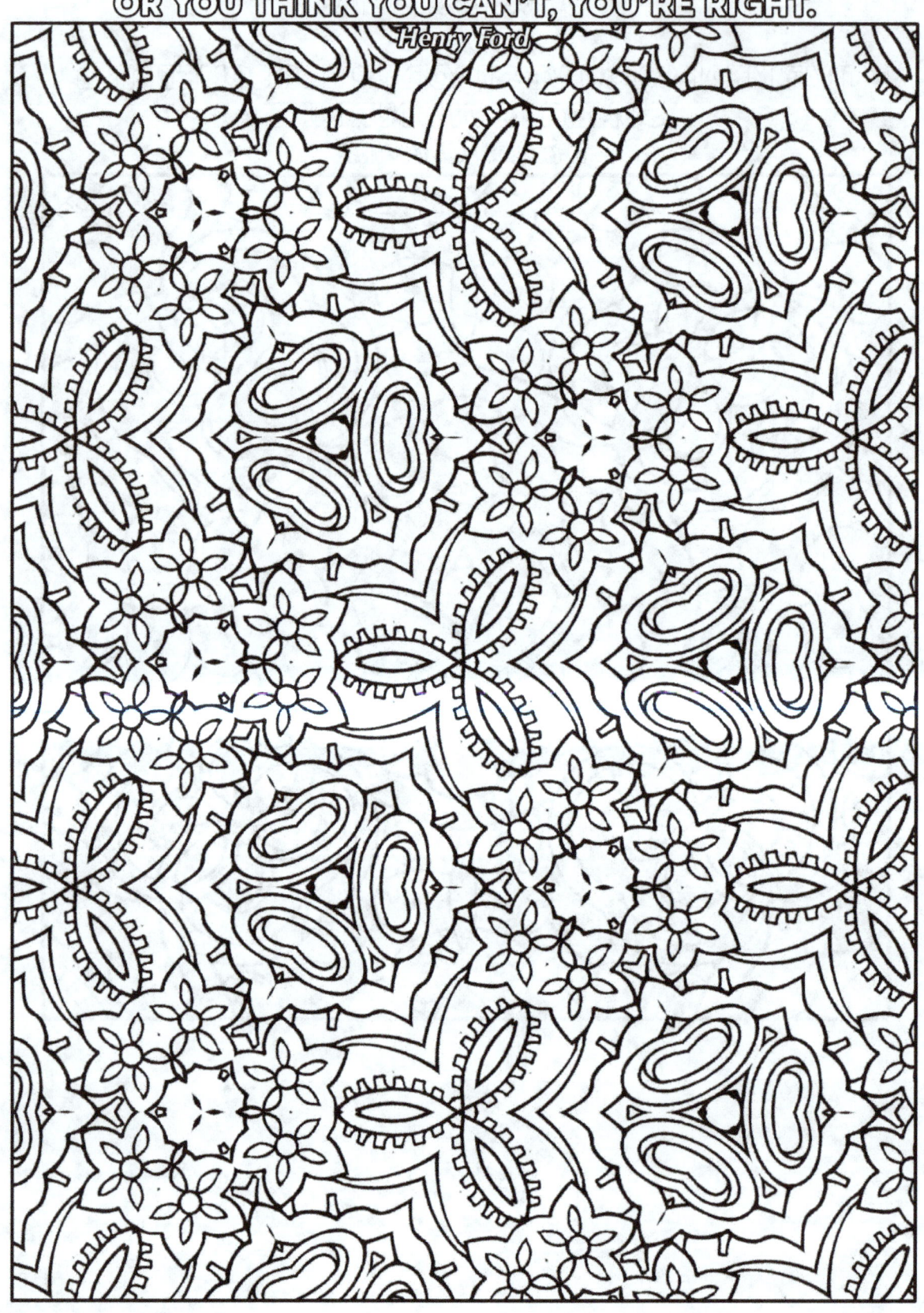

LIFE IS WHAT HAPPENS TO YOU
WHILE YOU'RE BUSY MAKING OTHER PLANS.
John Lennon

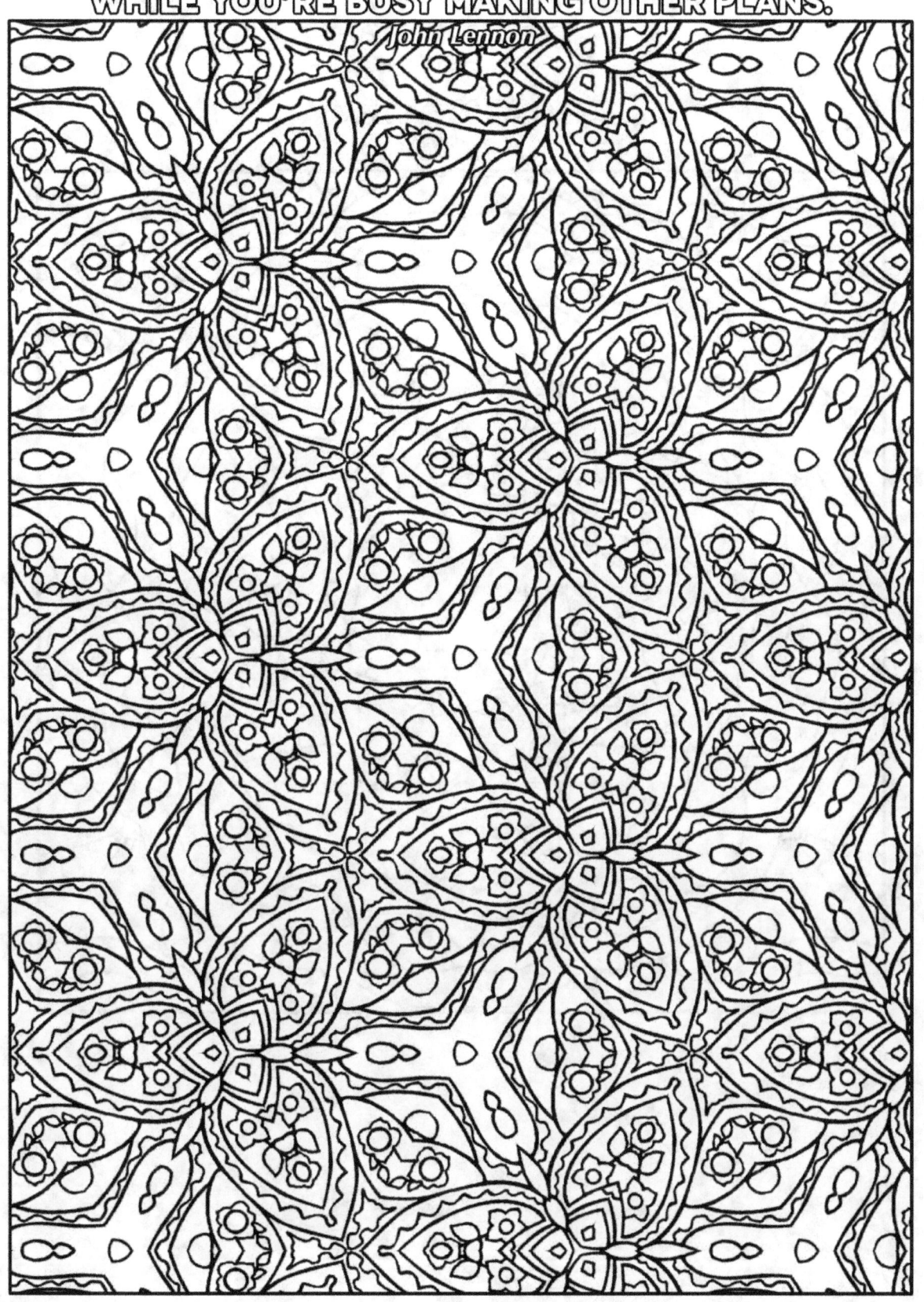

THERE IS ONLY ONE WAY TO AVOID CRITICISM:
DO NOTHING,
SAY NOTHING,
AND BE NOTHING.
Aristotle

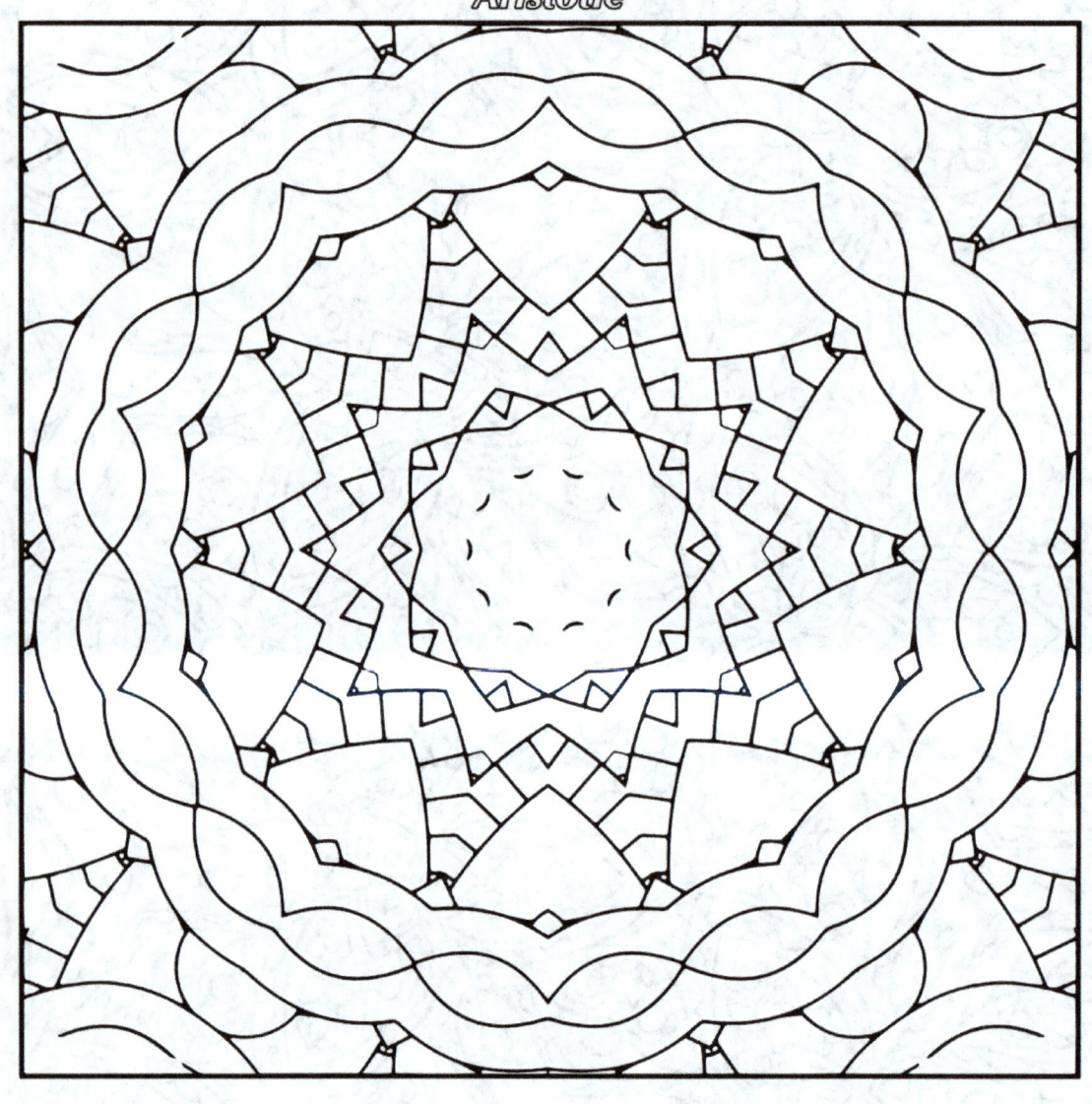

CERTAIN THINGS CATCH YOUR EYE, BUT PURSUE ONLY THOSE THAT CAPTURE THE HEART.

Ancient Indian Proverb

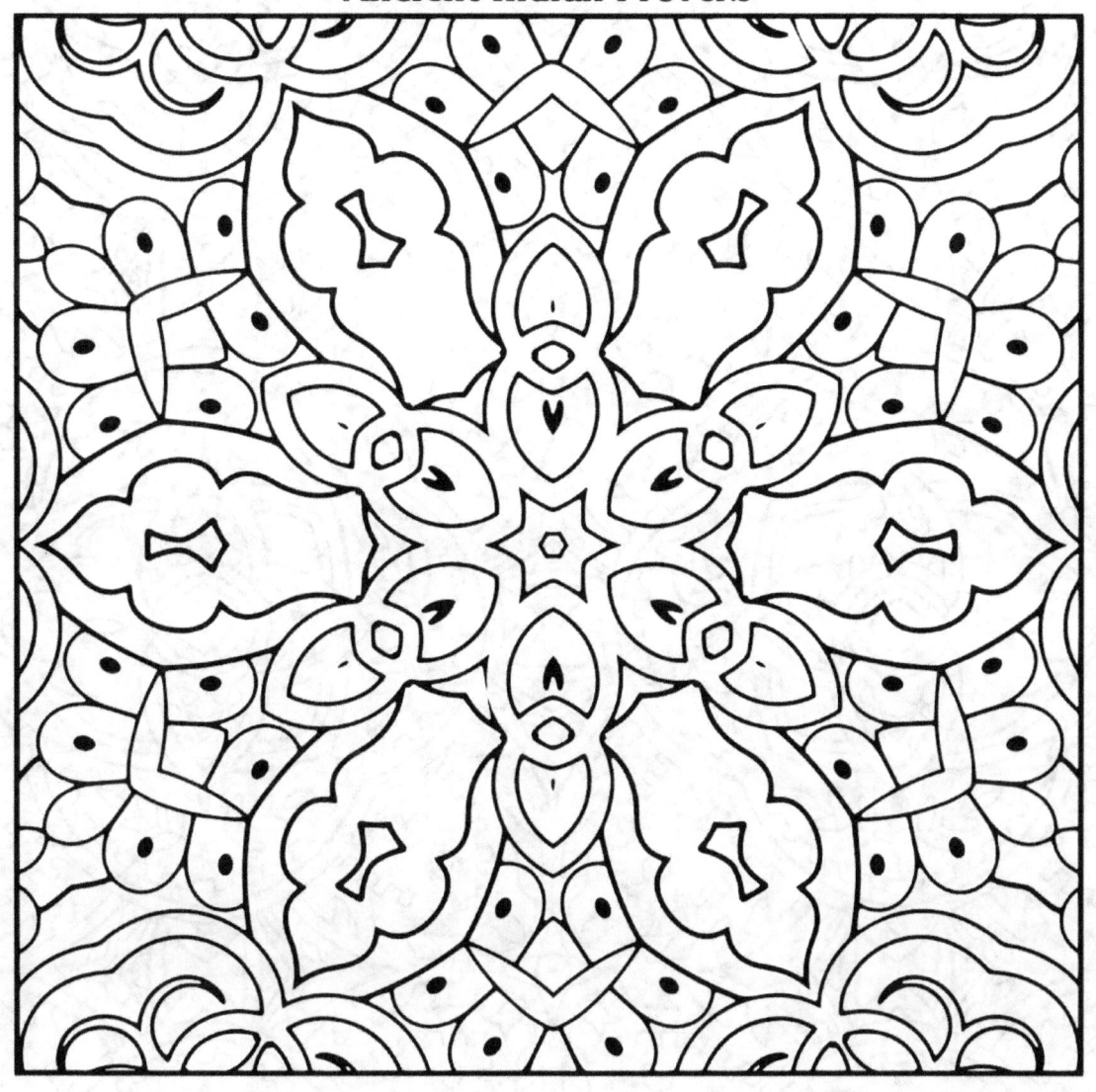

STRIVE NOT TO BE A SUCCESS,
BUT RATHER TO BE OF VALUE.
Albert Einstein

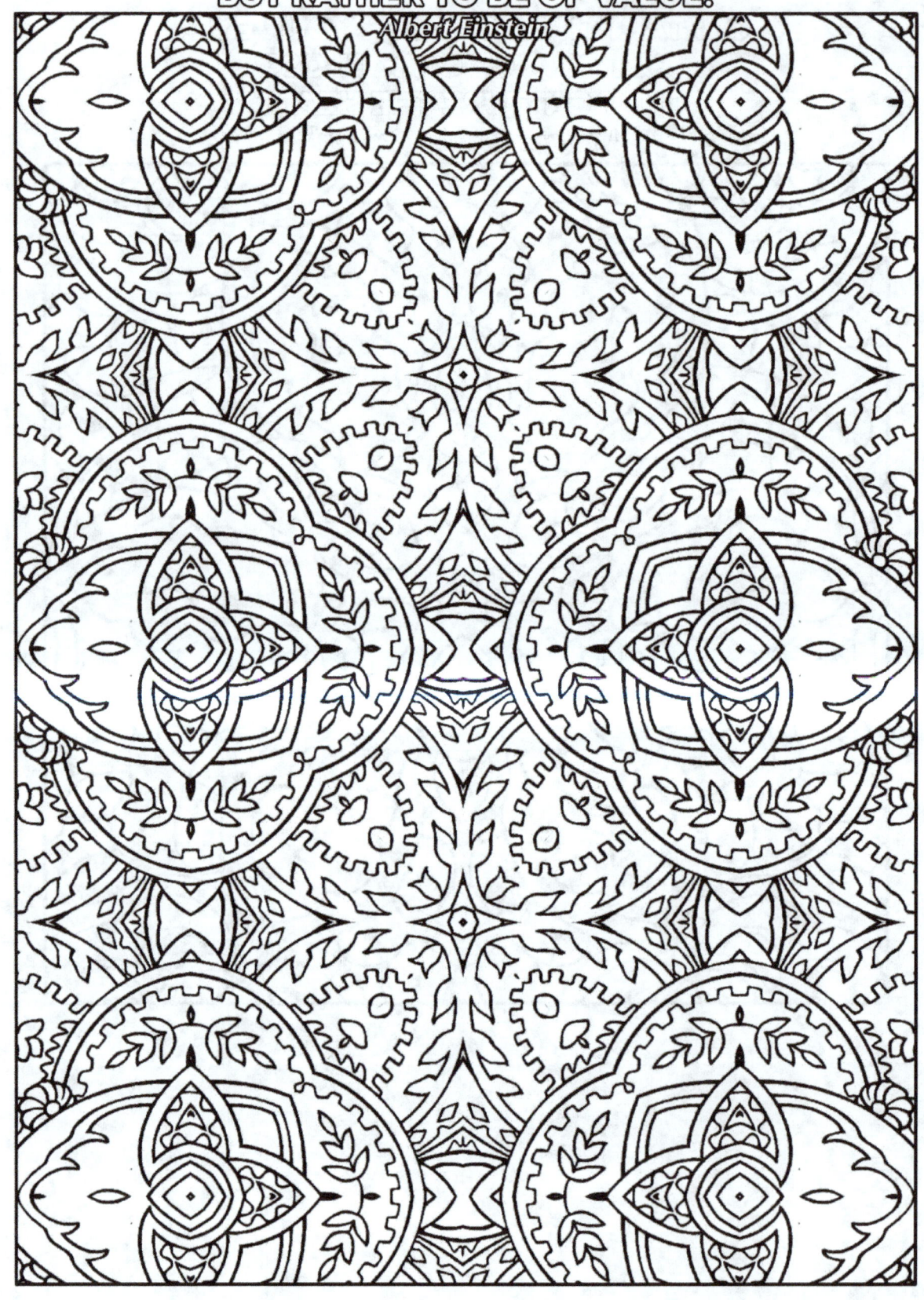

WHATEVER THE MIND OF MAN CAN CONCEIVE
AND BELIEVE, IT CAN ACHIEVE.
Napoleon Hill

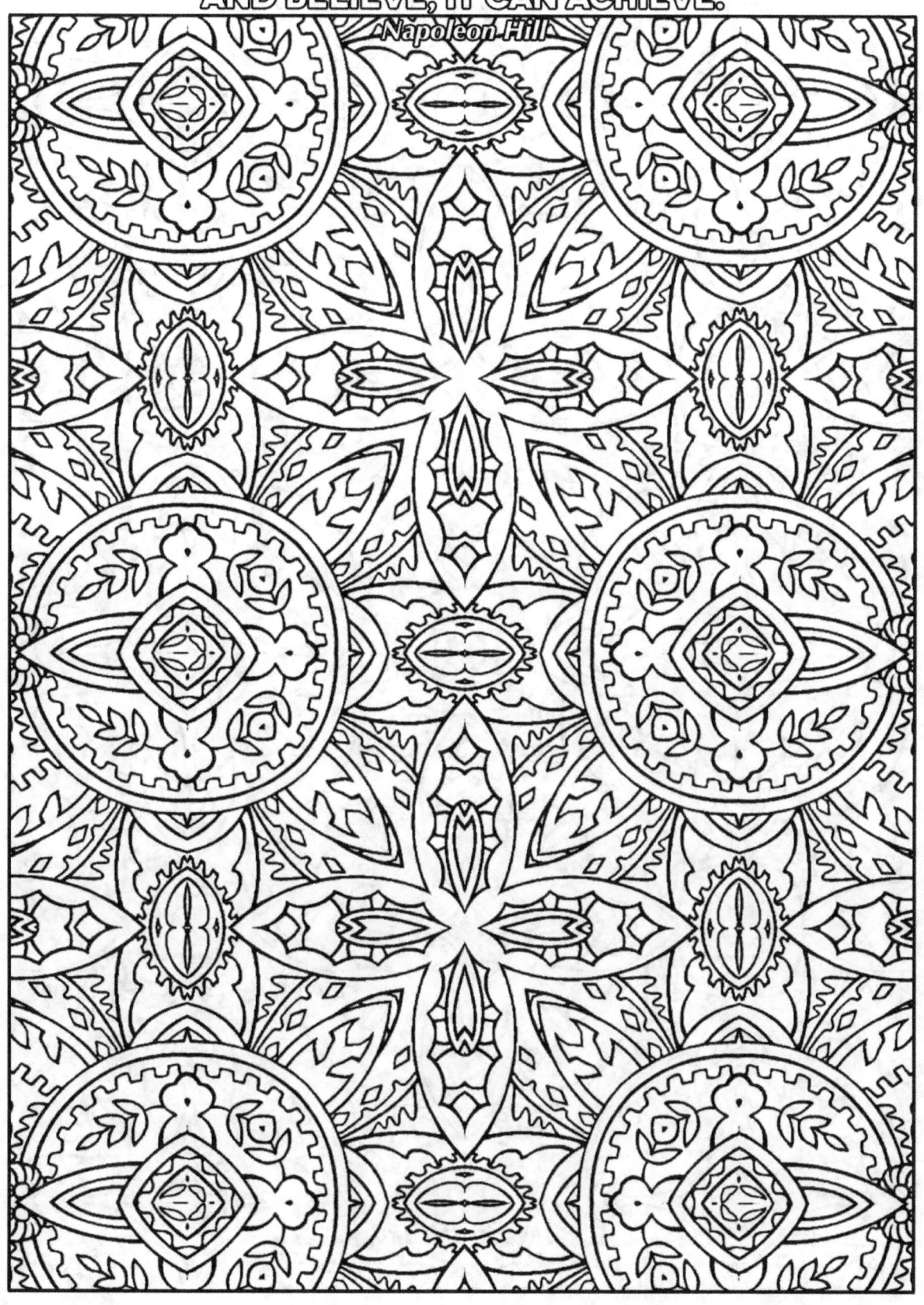

LIFE ISN'T ABOUT GETTING AND HAVING, IT'S ABOUT GIVING AND BEING.

Kevin Kruse

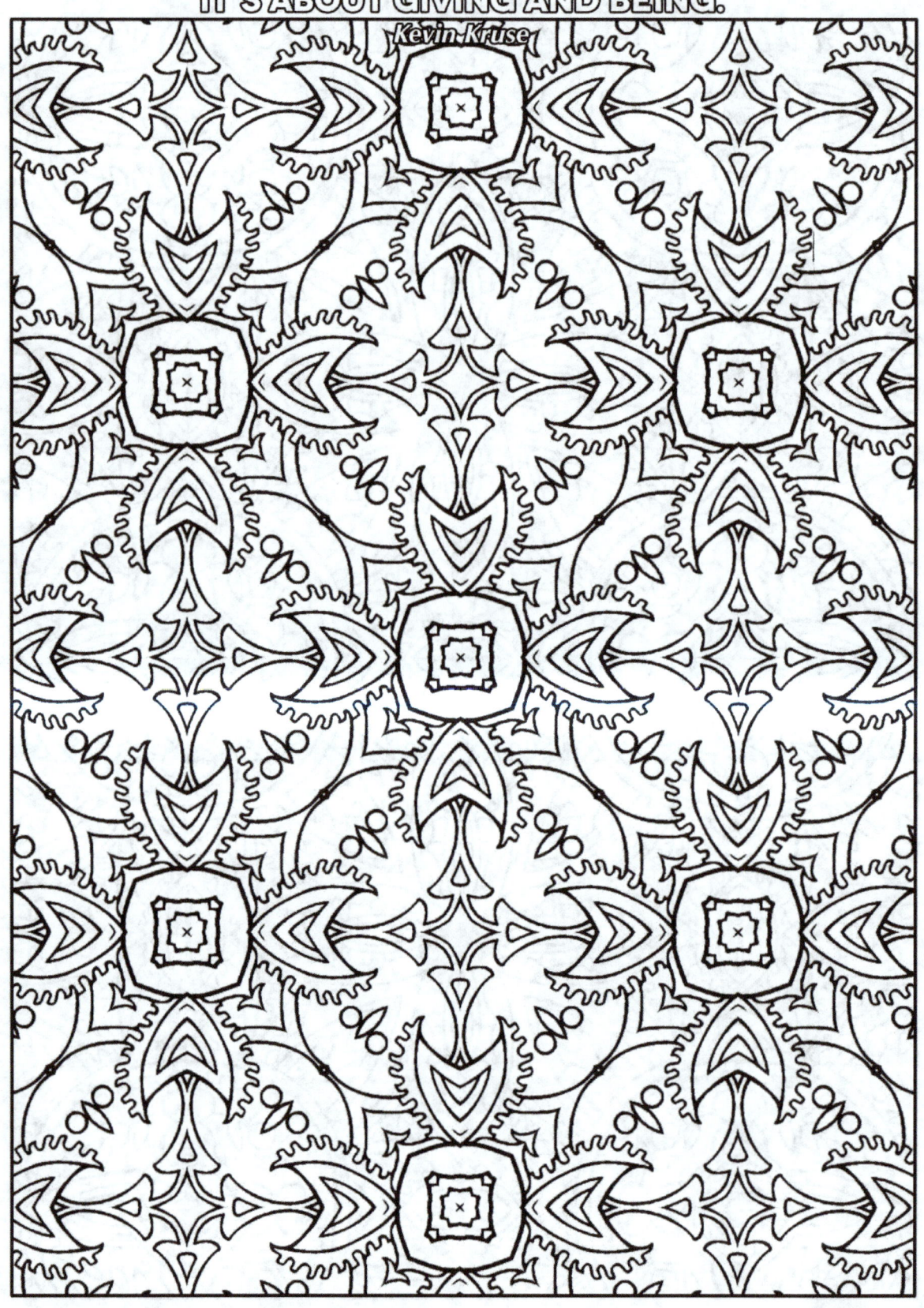

NOTHING IS IMPOSSIBLE, THE WORD ITSELF SAYS, "I'M POSSIBLE!"

Audrey Hepburn

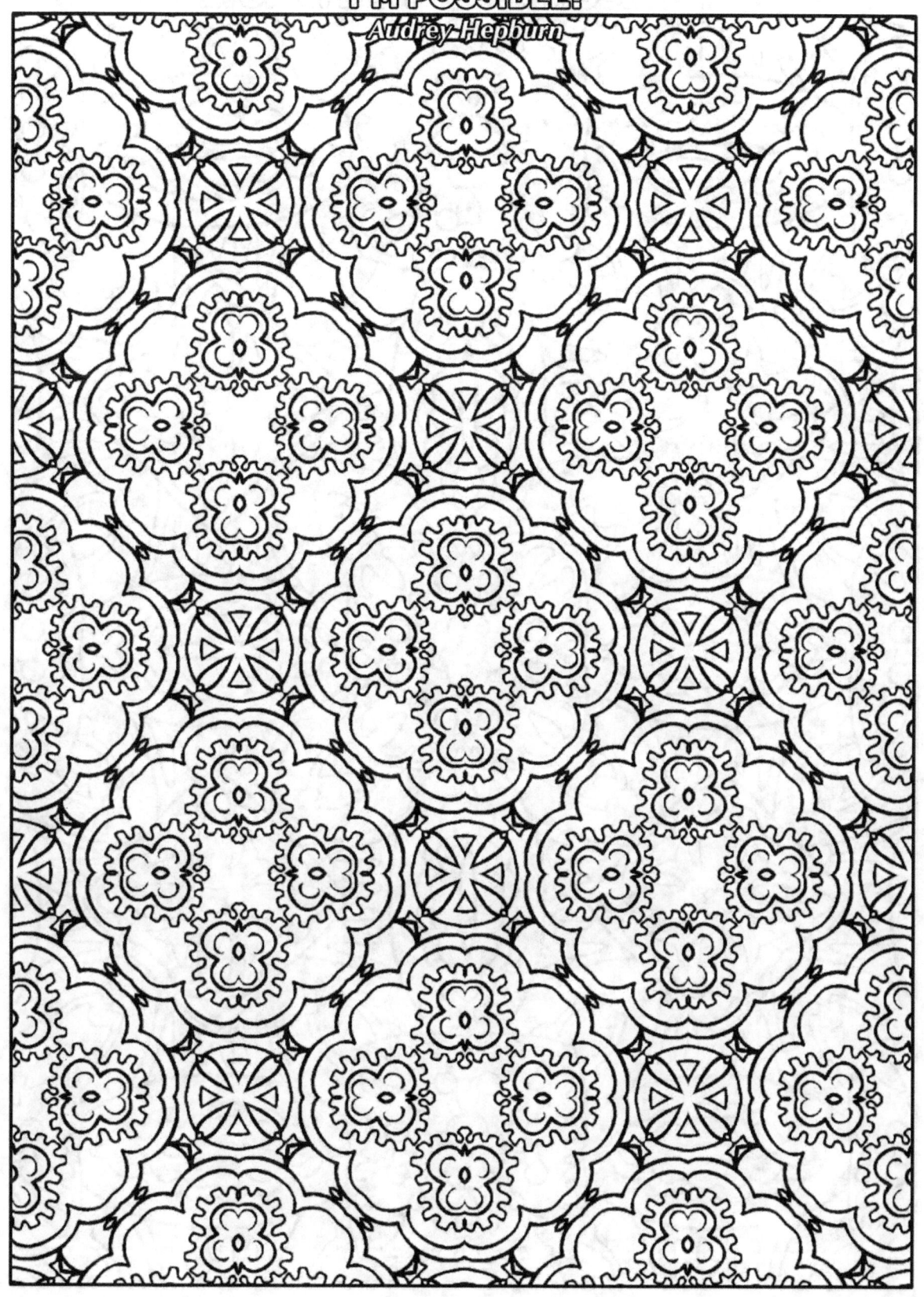

THE BEST TIME TO PLANT A TREE WAS 20 YEARS AGO.
THE SECOND BEST TIME IS NOW.

Chinese Proverb

IF YOU DO WHAT YOU'VE ALWAYS DONE,
YOU'LL GET WHAT YOU'VE ALWAYS GOTTEN.
Tony Robbins

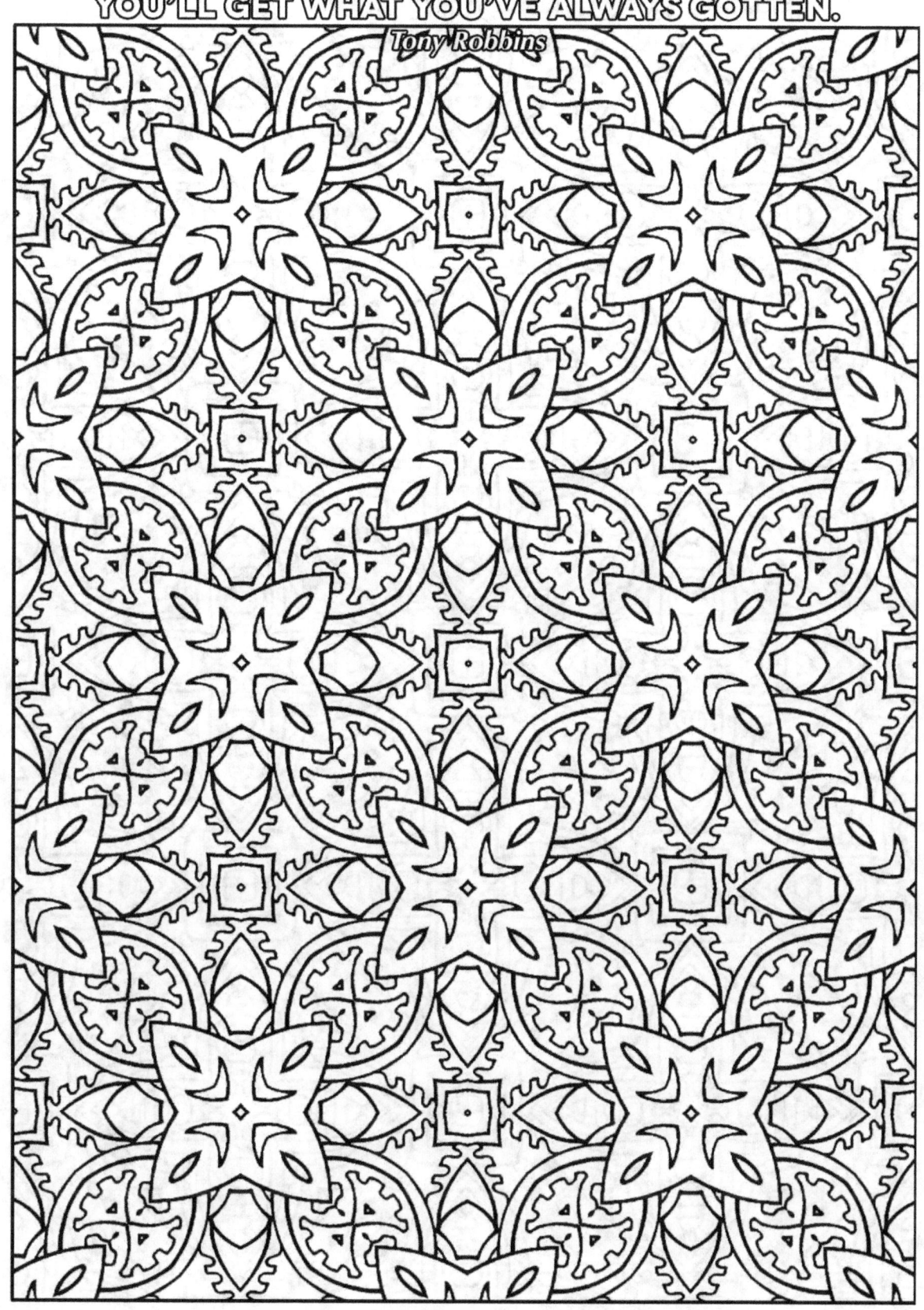

**YOU CAN'T USE UP CREATIVITY.
THE MORE YOU USE, THE MORE YOU HAVE.**
Maya Angelou

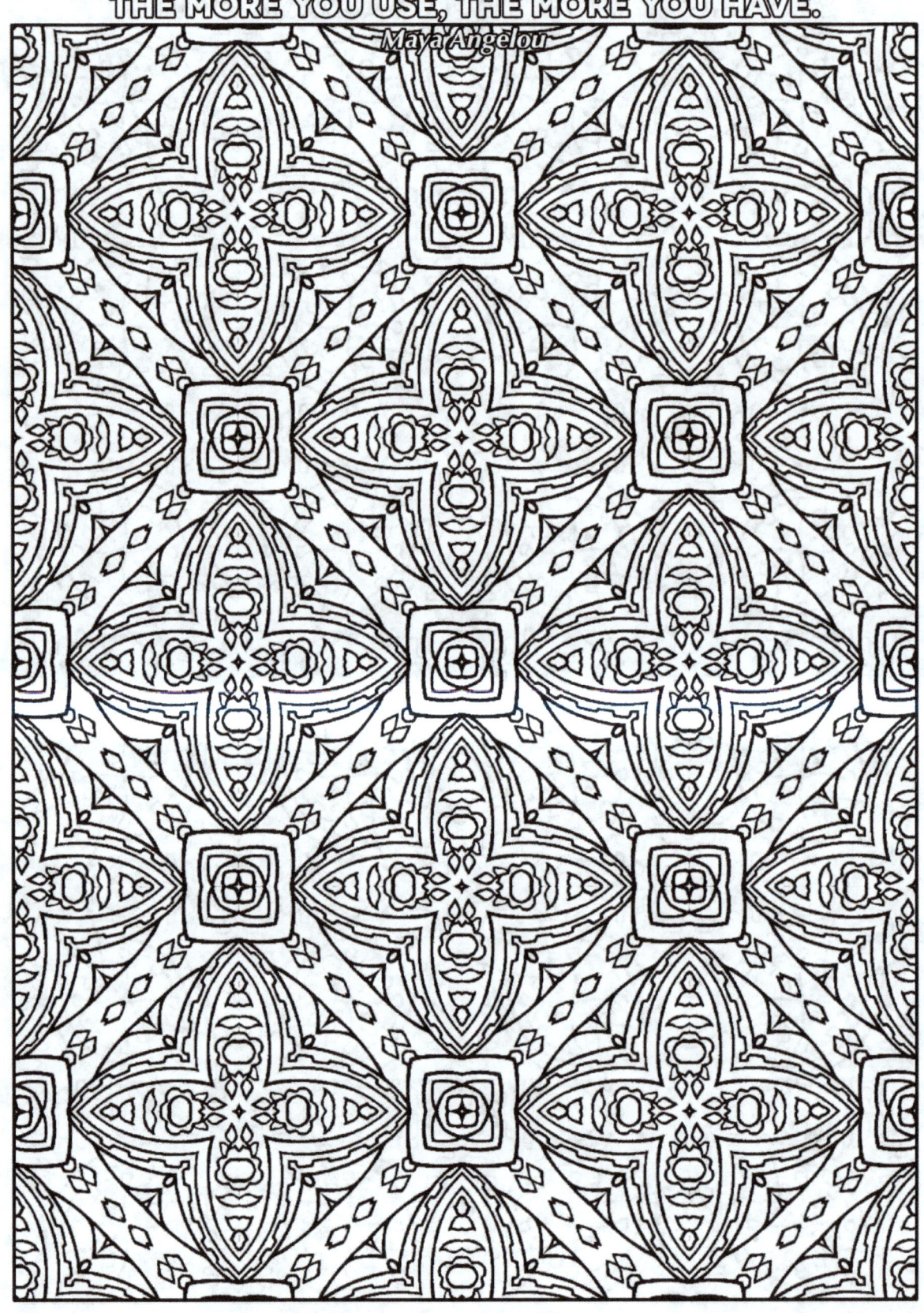

THE QUESTION ISN'T WHO IS GOING TO LET ME;
IT'S WHO IS GOING TO STOP ME.
Ayn Rand

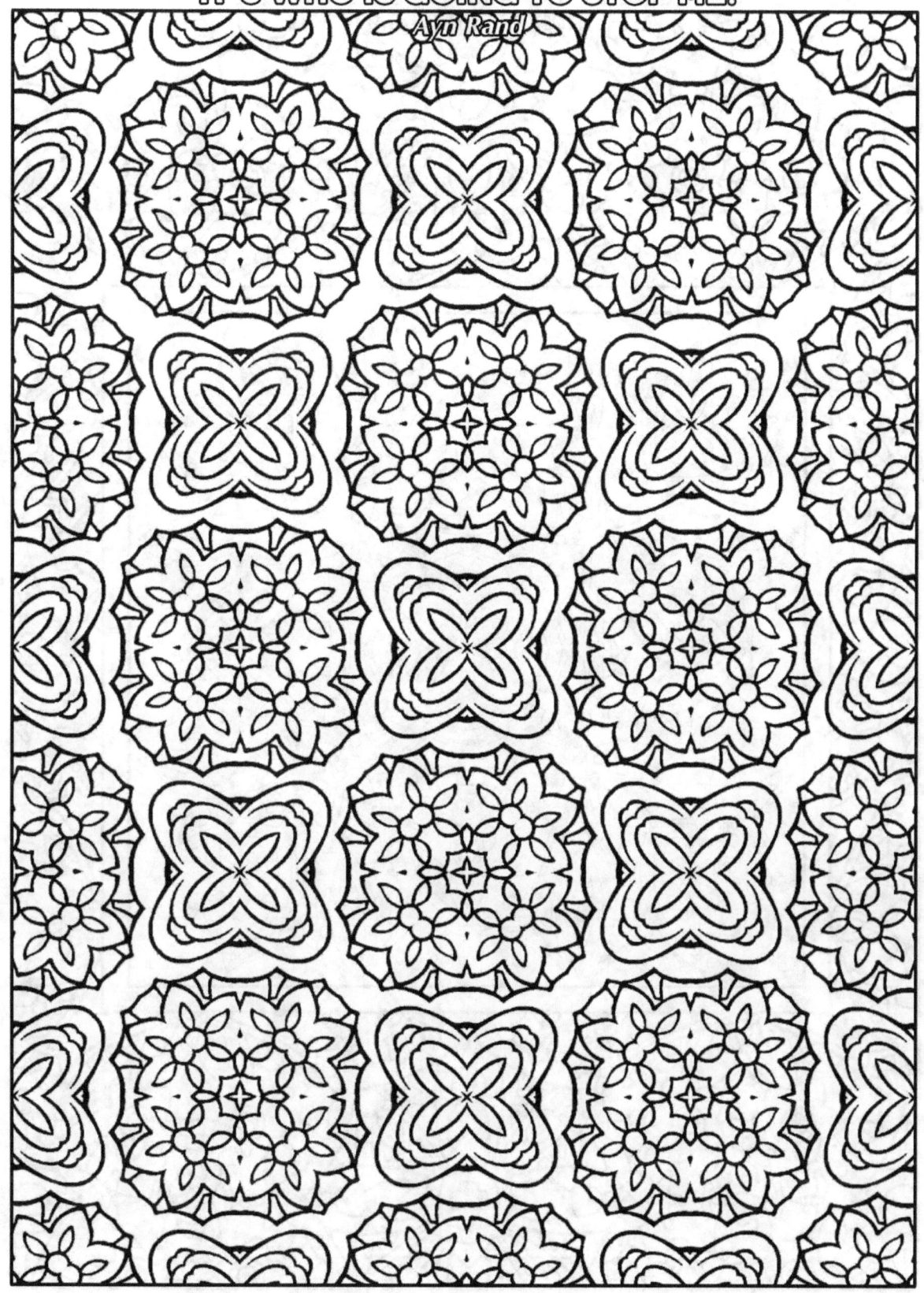

DEFINITENESS OF PURPOSE
IS THE STARTING POINT OF ALL ACHIEVEMENT.
W. Clement Stone

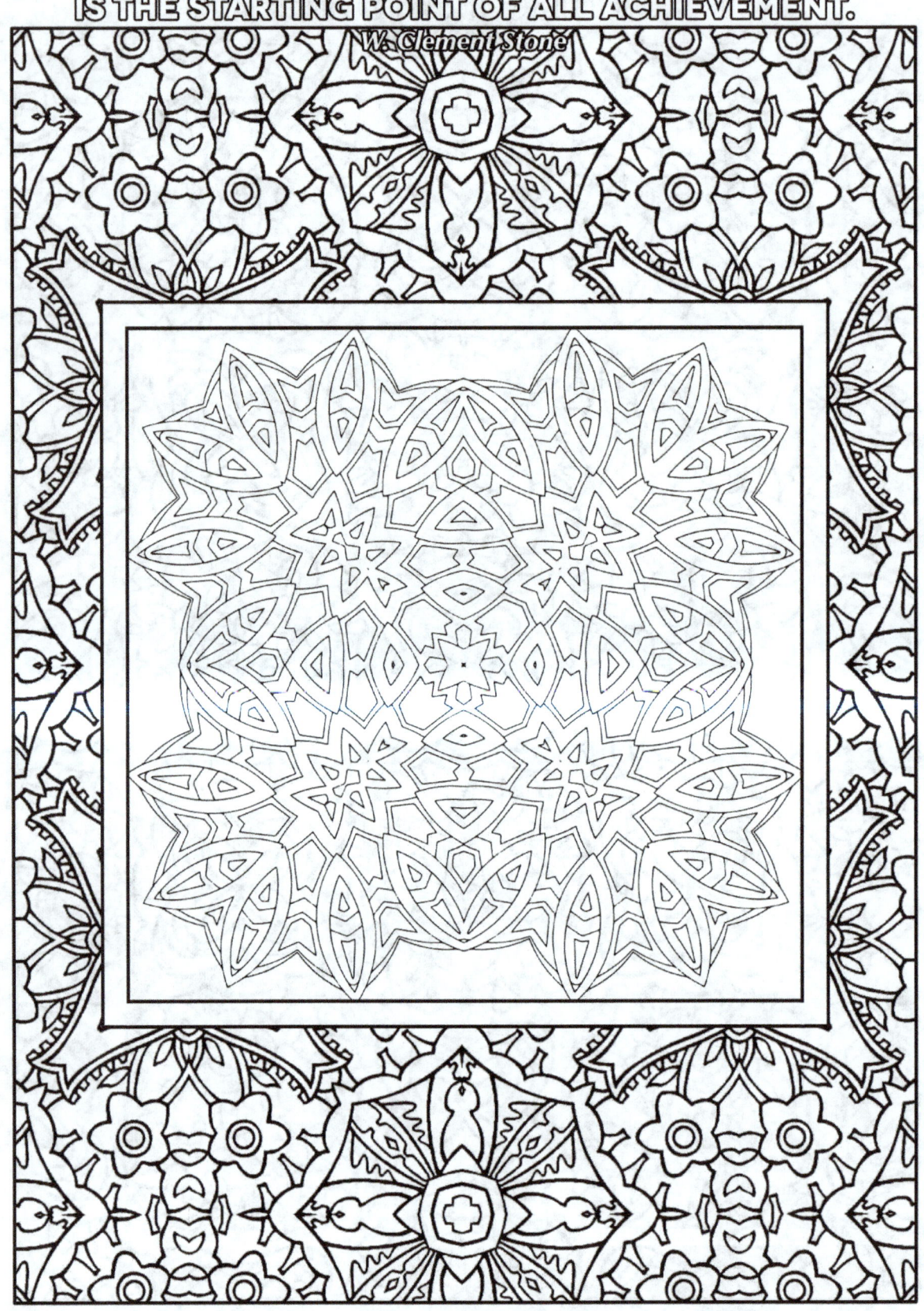

HAPPINESS IS NOT SOMETHING READYMADE.
IT COMES FROM YOUR OWN ACTIONS.

Dalai-Lama

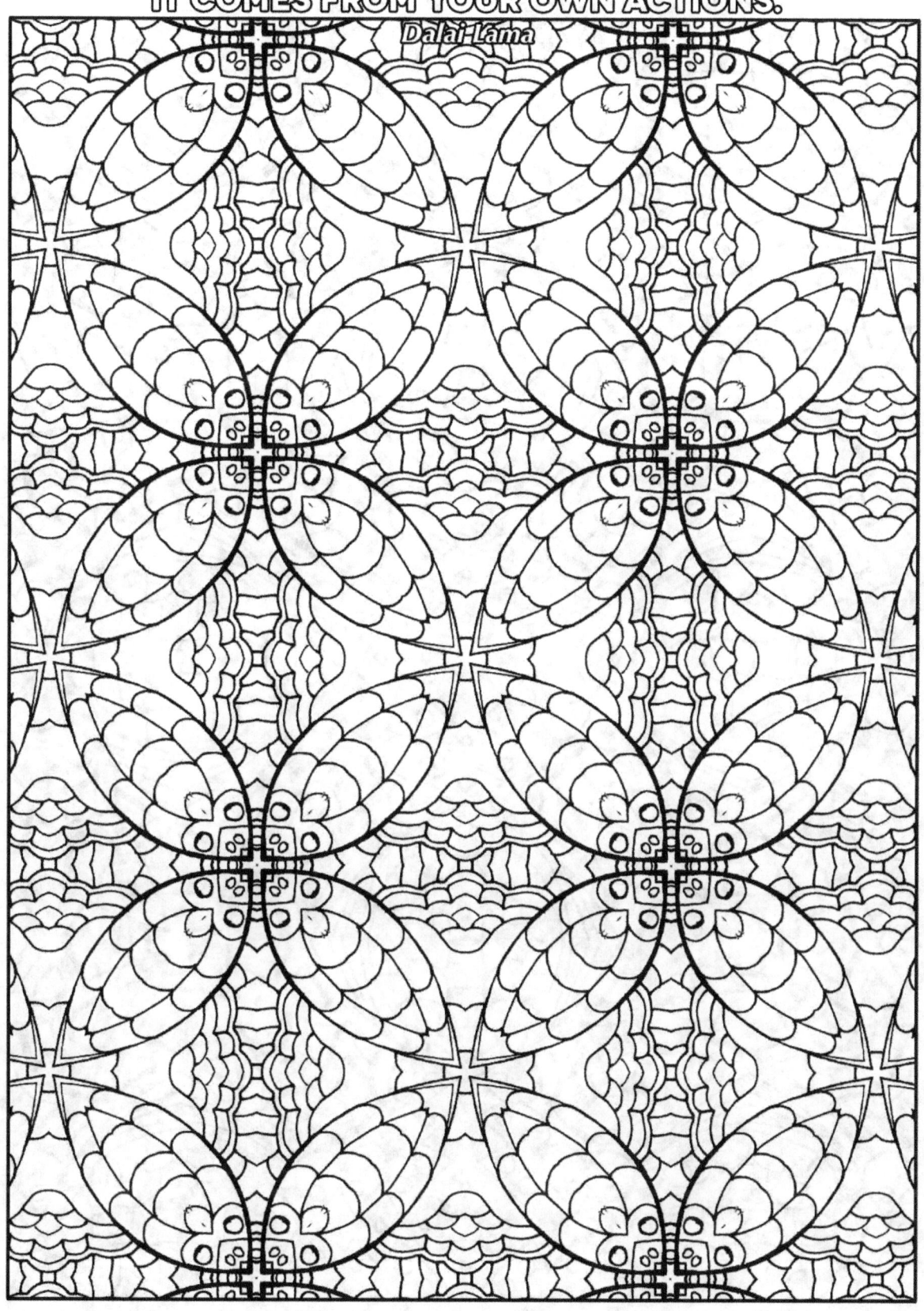

THE ONLY PERSON YOU ARE DESTINED TO BECOME
IS THE PERSON YOU DECIDE TO BE.
Ralph Waldo Emerson

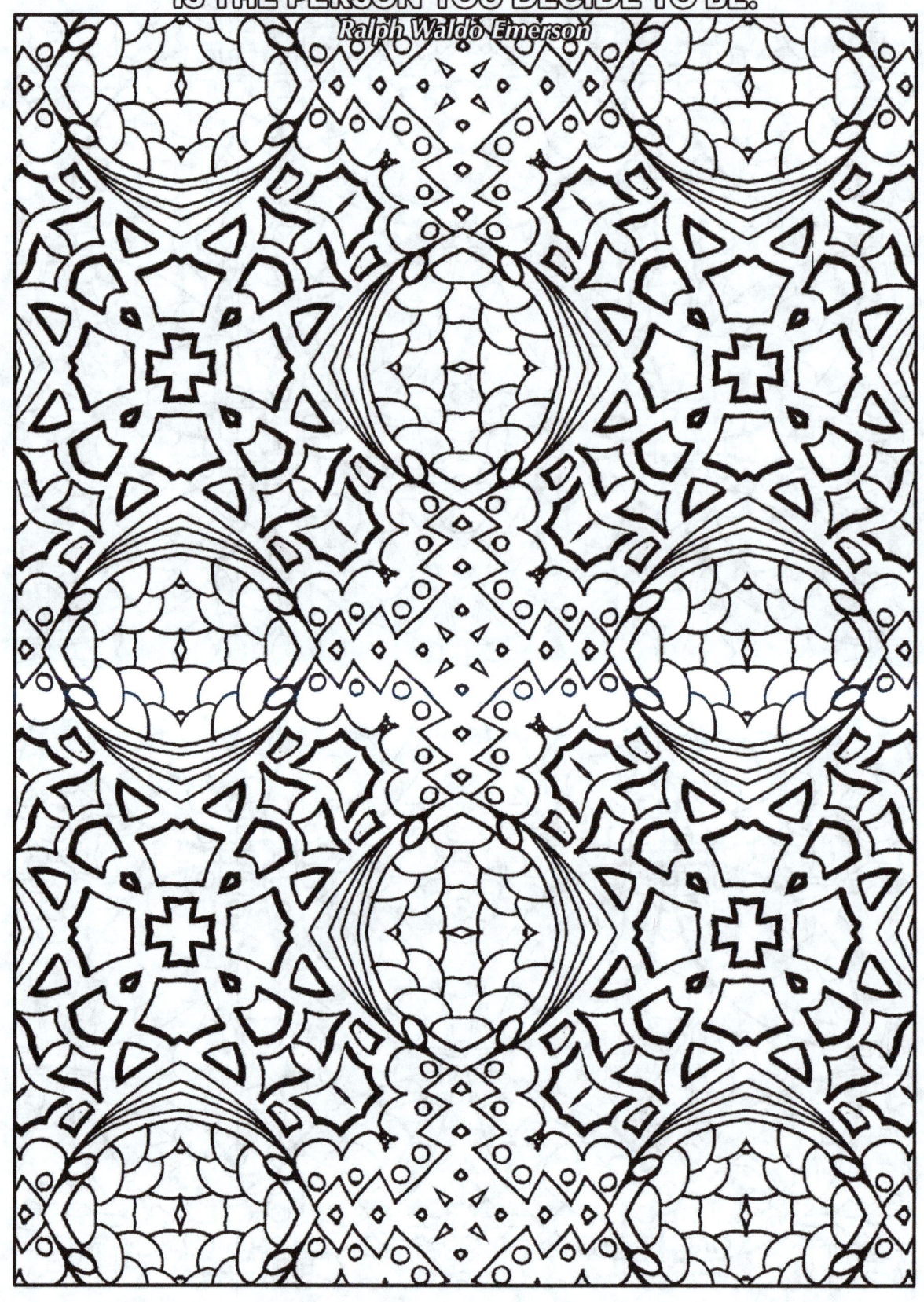

THE BEST WAY TO FIND YOURSELF
IS TO LOSE YOURSELF
IN THE SERVICE OF OTHERS.
Mahatma Gandhi

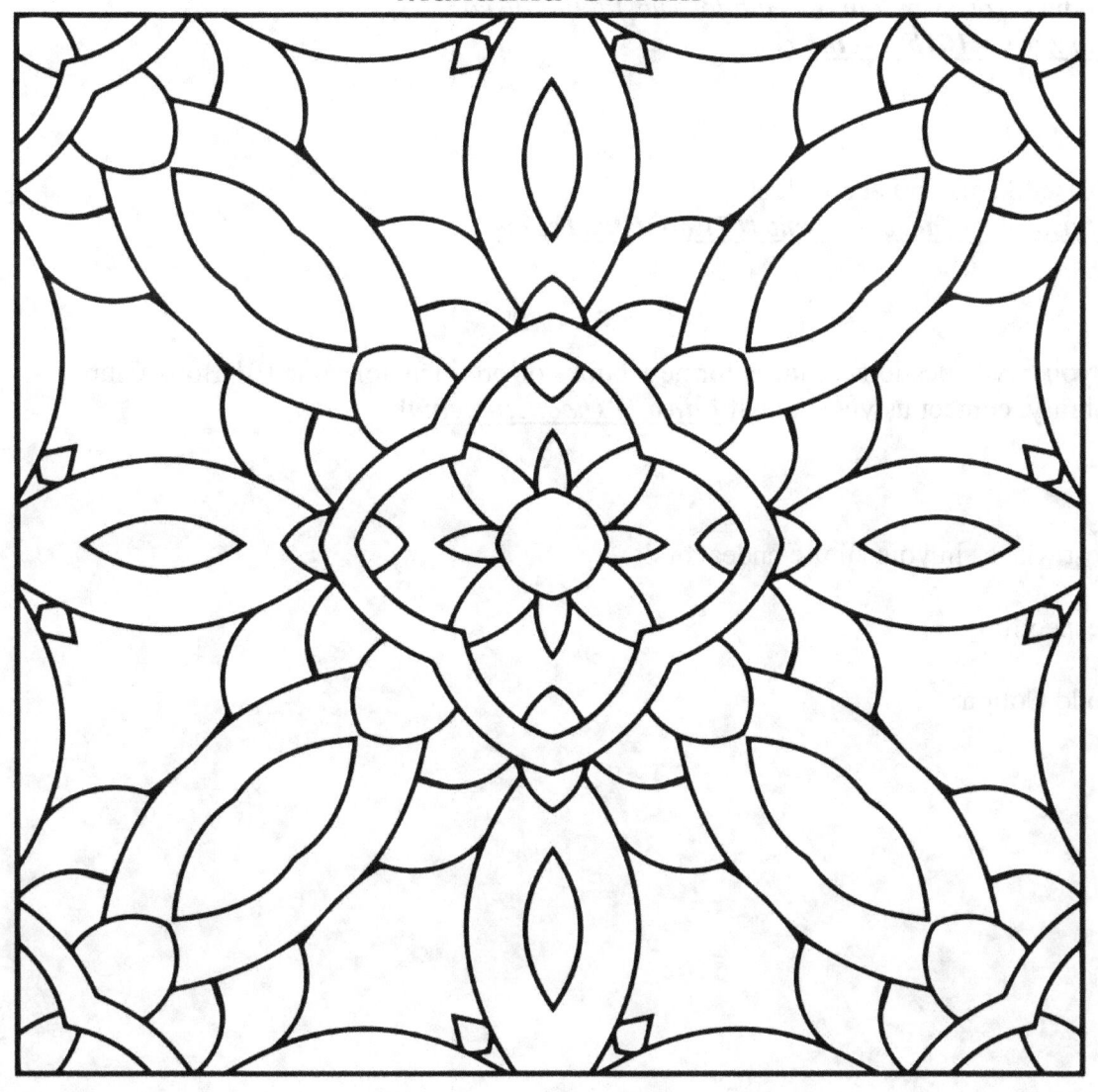

101 INSPIRATIONAL COLORING PATTERNS
Curated by Todd Cotton

If you enjoyed this book, you can learn more about our ever-growing library of books and products (*or even join the club for substantial discounts!*) at:
http://www.101bookclub.com/

Please like us on Facebook at:
https://www.facebook.com/101BookClubTeam/

If you have questions or ideas for new books or products for your 101 Book Club Library, contact us via email at **_info@101bookclub.com_**!

Best wishes in your future endeavors!

Respectfully,

Todd Cotton

If you enjoyed this book, we think you will LOVE our 101 Bible Heroes Coloring Book! Check it out at *http://www.101bookclub.com/* .

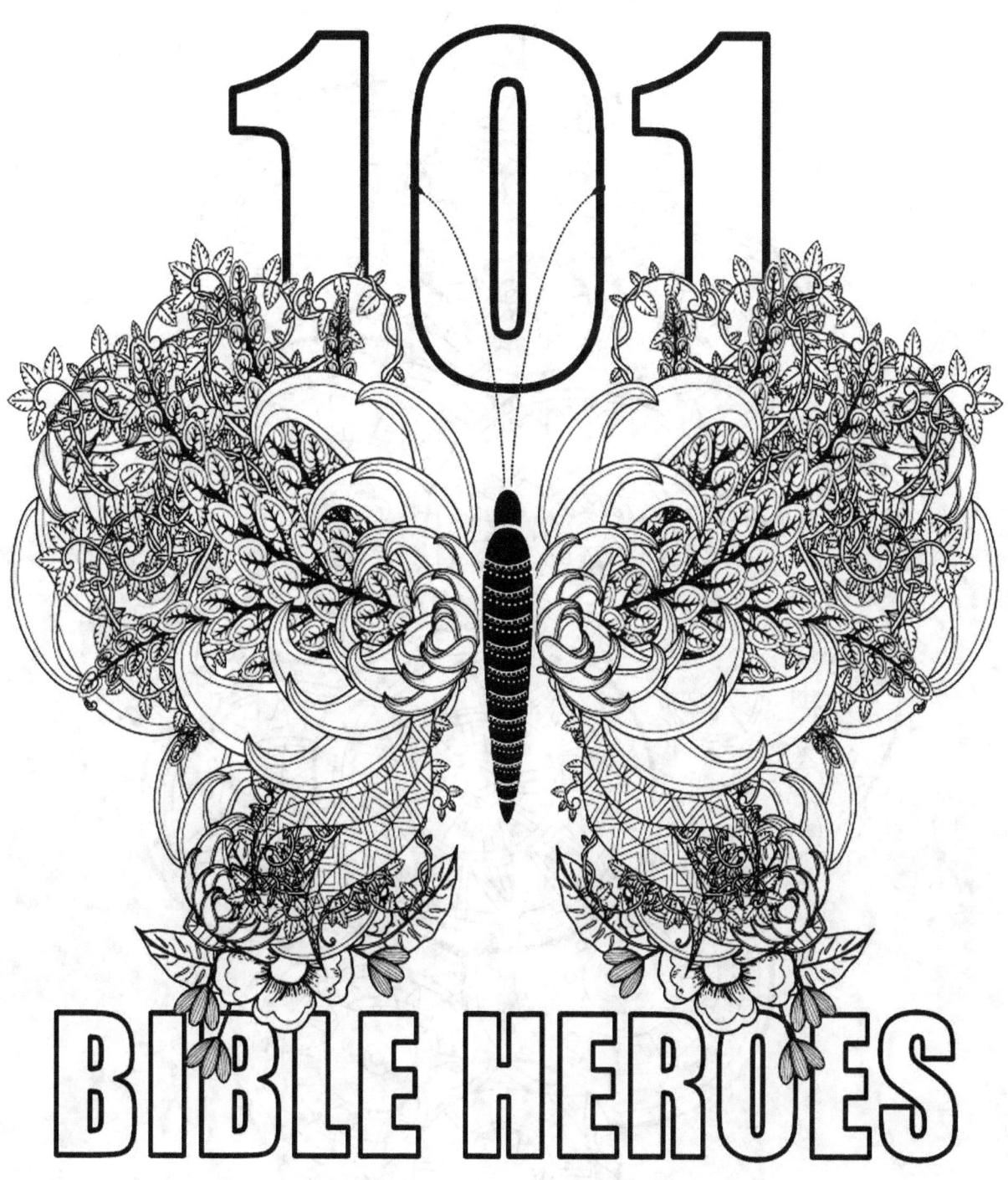

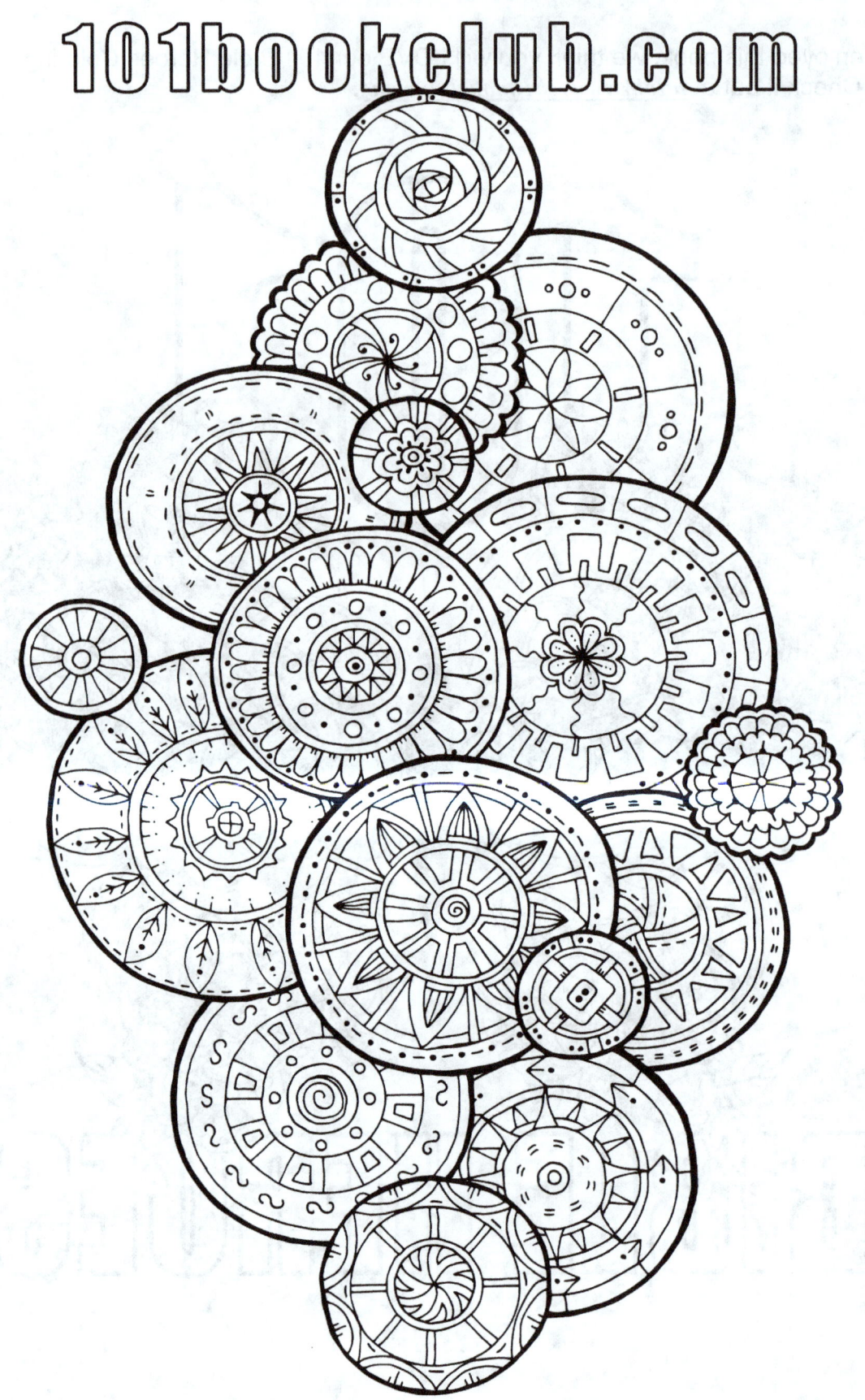

www.ingramcontent.com/pod-product-compliance
Lightning Source LLC
Chambersburg PA
CBHW081158180526
45170CB00006B/2139